GOD'S
Prosperity

Michaela Cooke

Order this book online at www.trafford.com
or email orders@trafford.com

Most Trafford titles are also available at major online book retailers.

Bible quotations are taken from the King James (version) of the Holy Bible.

Webster's New World Dictionary (Concise edition) Copyright 1973 by The Southwestern Company

Printed in the United States of America.

ISBN: 978-1-4269-9571-2 (sc)
ISBN: 978-1-4269-9570-5 (hc)
ISBN: 978-1-4269-9569-9 (e)

Library of Congress Control Number: 2012914892

Trafford rev. 12/11/2012

 www.trafford.com

North America & international
toll-free: 1 888 232 4444 (USA & Canada)
phone: 250 383 6864 ♦ fax: 812 355 4082

CONTENTS

ACKNOWLEDGEMENTS

I would like to acknowledge and thank:

Sarah Cooke;

She was the one who first brought me back into completing the book. It took years to finally get up enough nerve to tell the church, in plain English, God and Jesus' viewpoints on life. Thus, out of being discouraged; I had given up and just decided to throw the book aside. Sarah took a little over five months out of her lunch and spare time, to retype what had been written and presented it to me as a Christmas gift. The Holy Spirit used Sarah to snap me back into grasping God and Jesus' desire to get the truth out to Their people. And this book was born.

Sonja Meiners;

She was the person who proof read and drew my attention to lessons that were not explained clear enough. Thank God for her spelling and proper English ability. I would not have gotten through without her help. She works with legal contracts all day long, thank God for Sonja!

Danielle and Joshua LaBorde;

They both helped me with the Bible Scriptures recorded in each of the chapters. They made sure that they were put down correctly.

David and David Cooke;

David, my son, and David, my husband, both have inspired me and helped by suggesting ways to express Jesus' truths. David, my son, read each chapter with me and helped express Jesus' truths in younger and more up-to-date expressions. My husband was impressed by the Holy Spirit to help with the backup work which goes on behind the lines.

Each and every one of these people has been a BIG, and I do mean a BIG, blessing in my life. And it is only God who can thank them properly. I cannot! Praise God!!

Author

Since it was the Holy Spirit who wrote this book through me, I cannot claim I am the only author of "God's Prosperity". But as the title page indicates, I did fashion and put the Holy Spirit's words on the page as I received them in my Spirit.

If you are interested, I am a housewife who home-schooled three children. God has caused me to live through every message taught in the manuscript. But, my husband is still learning God and Jesus' lessons; therefore, we are not where God wants us to be as yet, but: I can testify this much: As David is improving with these lessons, our lives are improving financially. We are better off then we have ever been before! Praise God!!

INTRODUCTION

You need to know, it is the Holy Spirit who has written this entire book through me.

> *"But the Comforter, which is the Holy Ghost, whom the Father will send in my name, he shall teach you all things, and bring all things to your remembrance, whatsoever I have said unto you."*

> John 14:26

> *"Howbeit when he, the Spirit of truth, is come he will guide you into all truth: for he shall not speak of himself; but whatsoever he shall hear, that shall he speak: and he will shew you things to come. He shall glorify me: for he shall receive of mine, and shall shew it unto you."*

> John 16:13-14

It is not up to me to convince you that it actually was the Holy Spirit who wrote this book; but God said that **He** would be the **One who would prove these facts to you.**

> "And Moses said unto God, Behold, when I come unto the children of Israel, and shall say unto them, The God of your fathers hath sent me unto you; and they shall say to me, What is his name? what shall I say unto them? And

God said unto Moses, I AM THAT I AM: and he said, Thus shalt thou say unto the children of Israel, I AM hath sent me unto you."

Exodus 3:13-14

"This is He that came by the water and blood, even Jesus Christ, not by water only, but by water and blood. And it is the Spirit that beareth WITNESS, because the Spirit is truth."

I John 5:6

Here are some guidelines that will let you know if it is the Holy Spirit, *OR NOT.*

First of all, **I John 4:1-3** lets us know we must be total believers in the Lord, Jesus Christ. And we must totally believe that He died on the cross in our place. In other words, we must believe in and on God's Son, Y'shua (**Isaiah Ch. 53**). (Here is a revelation for you. It is only the Spirit of God who can reveal who Jesus really is, **I Corinthians 12:3**).

Secondly, **I Corinthians 2:11-16** lets us know that God has given us His Holy Spirit, in the world and on the inside of our bodies. And if the words written *do agree* totally with your God-given Spirit, which resides on the inside of you, then you can know that it is the Holy Spirit who is guiding/writing these truths (**I John 4:5-6 & 5:6-9**).

Thirdly, **Psalm 67:2** tells us that God's ways can be known by mere men and women.

"__He made known his ways unto Moses,__ his acts unto the children of Israel."

Psalms 103:7

And fourthly, the words written have more than just one Chapter and Bible reference which is used, to back up the point that is being made.

"__But if he will not hear thee, then take with thee one or two__ __more, that in the mouth of two or three witnesses every word__ __may be established."__

Matthew 18:16

This fact is also recorded in **Numbers 35:30; Deuteronomy 19:15; John 8:17** & **II Corinthians 13:1**. All through the book you will find both the Old and New Testament scriptures to substantiate the positions being taught. Only the Holy Spirit has the ability to bring this kind of scripture to memory (**John 14:26; John 16:13-14** & **Deuteronomy 18:18-22**).

We are not here to discuss whether the facts in the book are true or false. This is not my work. It belongs to the Holy Spirit (**John 16:8-11**). Thus, there are several ways to read it for the best results in your life. You may not want to follow the Holy Spirit's instructions, but following them sure helped me.

First, read the book by looking up the scriptures as you read. Without the scriptures to back up the points given, the book is just words put on paper. But, I have noticed when I took the time to look up the scriptures the Holy Spirit gave; sometimes I lost the truths being given. So, the Holy Spirit impressed me to read the book again, but this time He suggested scanning the references only and not looking them up.

He told me to tell you; remain quiet for a while, and let Him deal with you on the facts written (meditate). Then go back and read the book again. But this time, take the opportunity to study and meditate on the information presented. Unless we understand the scriptures from God and Jesus' viewpoints, we will never be able to prosper with Them (**Deuteronomy 8:18, Hosea 2:8, Ezekiel 16:17-19 & Proverbs 13:28**). Read these scriptures in this order, they will speak to you.

It is a known fact, even in Satan's world, you MUST hear the SAME facts at least SEVEN times before the human mind begins to understand, take in, and believe the instructions given. You are welcome to try to prove these lessons wrong if you desire to do so, but God's words always stand true.

Once you do believe Jesus and His words (**John 12:48**); and you start to think the way that He thinks, then you are on your way to having **John 10:10** fulfilled in your life (**Proverbs 23:7**).

My prayer for you is **Matthew 13:15**.

> *"For this people's heart is waxed gross, and their ears are dull of hearing, and their eyes they have closed; lest at any time they should see with their (Spiritual) eyes, and hear with their (Spiritual) ears, and should understand with their (Spiritual) heart, and should be converted* (Isaiah 55:6-11 & **Ephesians 4:19-25**), *and I should heal them."*

> **Matthew 13:15**

May the GOOD LORD bless each and every one of His people!!

CHAPTER 1

Our Tithes

THE LORD HAS IMPRESSED me to write you about one teaching which has been a sore spot in the church for a very long time—your tithes and offerings. When it comes to money, it becomes very personal and difficult to get the church body to tithe. Did you know it is a proven fact; only one-tenth of any given church congregation will tithe faithfully?

Frankly, with the teachings on our tithes and offerings, I can see why. It used to bother me to give away money I thought (and felt as if) I would never see again. When I paid my bills, at least I received a service for the money spent. But when it came to the church, it appeared as if it was only the ministries who were receiving the blessings being promised.

Before we go on, let's go over some of the scriptures which tell us to tithe. Then we will review the reasons why we are to give to God the first ten percent of our income. This means, we are to give to our church, to the poor, or to a ministry (as God directs us) one-tenth of our income. God and Jesus do require us to tithe, but most people have no idea as to why. Thus, we will tackle these reasons in this chapter. We will start with the scriptures which tell us to tithe.

Adam taught Cain and Able to bring a tithe offering to God during the time they lived on the outside of the Garden of Eden **(Genesis 4:1-5)**. In **Genesis 14:18-20**, Abram tithed to Melchizedek (king of Salem). ___Both of these tithings were required BEFORE the Mosaic Law ever went into effect___! Again, Jacob tithed to God, on all he had, ___before___ the terms of the Mosaic Law were ever set in place **(Genesis 28:22)**. This fact means: tithing is ___NOT just part of the Mosaic Law.___ It is required throughout scripture because God and Jesus want our hearts to be towards Them **(Jeremiah 7:21-23 & Matthew 6:19-21)**. Jesus' words are NOT suggestions. They are COMMANDMENTS. This fact means, Jesus doesn't suggest, but commands us to tithe to God **(Matthew 6:19-20 & 22:21)**.

> "They say unto him, Caesar's. Then saith he unto them, Render therefore unto Caesar the things which are Caesar's: ___and unto God the things that are God's___."

> Matthew 22:21

The tithe belongs' to God **(Leviticus 27:30 & Malachi 3:8-10)**.

> "And ___all the tithe___ of the land, whether of the seed of the land, or of the fruit of the tree, ___is the LORD'S___: it is holy unto the LORD."

> Leviticus 27:30

Therefore, as according to Jesus' commandment in **Matthew 6:19-20 & 22:21**, we are to render our tithe unto God. We also know that the Israelites were required to tithe in **Leviticus 27:30**.

Ecclesiastes Ch. 11 tells us to sow as well. This chapter explains to us; if we refuse to sow into God's Kingdom then there will be no way we can prosper. The evil is in this world (**Ecclesiastes 11:1-2**). Therefore, this evil can, and does eat the Christian's money which they received from the world. The only way we will not lose our income, is by sowing into God's Kingdom (**Matthew 6:19-20**).

We are told in **Malachi 3:8-9** if we withhold the tithe by using God's money for our own benefits, then we are robbing God because the tithe and offerings belong to Him. Thus, when we withhold the tithe and use it for our own benefits, we will lose our profits in other ways. Things will end up taking our money in ways we do not foresee. (Such as, you will need repairs on the dishwasher, or on the washing machine, or on the dryer when you are not expecting it to go out). (Or you get an unexpected bill, such as, your phone bill will end up being bigger then you anticipated). And I could go on and on. But I don't want to.

> "Will a man rob God? Yet ye have robbed me. But ye say, Wherein have we robbed thee? In tithes and offerings. Ye are cursed with a curse: for ye have robbed me, even this whole nation."

> **Malachi 3:8-9**

> "Ye have sown much, and bring in little; ye eat, but ye have not enough; ye drink, but ye are not filled with drink; ye clothe you, but there is none warm; and he that earneth wages, earneth wages to put it into a bag with holes."

> **Haggai 1:6**

To gain an understanding of **Haggai 1:6** read Chapter 1 of Haggai in its entirety. It will tell you, because you are not considering God's house, you have been cursed with a curse you cannot control.

Therefore, things will go wrong and eat your income. This is NOT just for the Israelites. Doesn't Jesus tell you in **Matthew 6:19**, moth and rust will corrupt your money? And thieves can and do break into your homes and steal your prosperity. These are the things which go wrong with the things you own. My family and I do tithe faithfully and are following Jesus' instructions as we learn them, so we are not cursed with these curses!

Our Lord gives us the answer as to why we are required to tithe. First and foremost, He tells us in **Matthew 6:19-20**, we are to sow into God's Kingdom (in other words, we are to tithe at least 10% of our money back to God). As a result, we will have a bank account in heaven. Whereby, God can prosper us. You cannot receive interest on money which isn't in your heavenly bank account. Secondly, He tells us to tithe so our hearts will be drawn towards heaven (**Matthew 6:21**). And the third, but not final reason, we are to tithe so we will not stand before God empty-handed. We are not allowed to stand before the kings and queens of this earth without a gift (**I Kings 10:1-2** & **Matthew 2:11**); so why would we disrespect God so much as to stand before **_Him_** empty-handed (**I Kings 10:1-2**; **Luke 7:1-5** & **Acts 10:1-4**)?

Very few people understand why God and Jesus do require us to tithe our money into Their Kingdom. Therefore, we will tackle this purpose now.

This is the way it works. You are told by Jesus in **Matthew 6:19-20** to lay up your treasure in heaven and not as much on this earth. In other words, you are to open up a bank account in heaven just as you do on this earth. You open it up by giving your tithe to God in the way He impresses you to give it to Him. Most people are impressed to give to a ministry.

Once you have obeyed Jesus' words in **Matthew 6:19-20,** the money you have sown into your account is just sitting there waiting on you. However, it cannot be drawn upon until you complete the requirements it takes to make the account active. If you refuse to sow, then there isn't any money in your account to withdraw when you are desperate. This is why you are told by Jesus to put at least 10% of your money into your heavenly account.

This fact is important to know; *the money you use to open your account and the money you deposit into your heavenly account will never be touched by thieves, rust, or moths.* In other words, when you put your money in your bank account, this money is yours and it is just as valuable as the day you deposited it (**Matthew 6:20**). But again, you are not allowed to draw on your financial credit until you perform the requirements it takes to activate your account. (This will be reemphasized in **Amos 5:11; Zephaniah 1:12-13; Deuteronomy 28:38-40; Joel 2:25-26 & Isaiah 65:21-22** later on in this chapter).

If you refuse to obey Jesus' words in **Matthew 6:19-20** by refusing to tithe any of your money into God's Kingdom, then there is no way you can receive anything from God or His Kingdom. This is true because of the natural law that was set into place when this world was created, and the same law exists to this very day. You do NOT receive anything unless you sow first.

The natural laws are different from the Mosaic Law. The natural laws govern our lives whether we want them to or not. For example, the law of gravity causes things to fall to the ground because it is a natural law which governs the world. In like manner, the natural law of sowing and reaping governs our lives whether we want it to or not. For example, you must sow into your employment by giving them your talents of doing the work, BEFORE you are allowed to receive a paycheck. If you do not believe me, go to work and ask your boss if he would be willing to give you one week's pay without you working for it, or earning a vacation. What do you think his answer would be?

"Sure, John or Jane, I don't think you're crazy, and I'll give you the money right away." What is the actual chance of this happening? You are required to sow your time, talents, expertise, and your blood, sweat and tears into your job before you are permitted to receive any money for your services. Many times, the pressure is on to give the company 110% of yourself *before* you are able to receive what you are worth.

This is why it is so hard to tithe. You have worked hard to receive what little you get in a paycheck. Thus, after you have paid your bills and taken care of your family, there is just something on the inside of you which says, "If there is anything left, I would sure like to save it for me". Yet there are times when you feel guilty and selfish for thinking this way, so every once in a while you drop some money in the offering bucket. But, again I know where you are coming from.

For a long time I have been upset with seeing the ministry people being the ones who get to help the hurting people in other countries, while I am sitting back and watching them do this act on television. I want to be a part of the fun. I also want to be able to help others personally from my heart. Oh, you can go if you come up with an extra $2,000 or $3,000, which is the requirement to pay your own way. How fair is that? The minister is going across seas on my money; and if I want to go, I must somehow come up with the additional funds to pay my own way. Needless to say, I have never made a mission trip.

The scriptures write about this situation. It says in **Amos 5:11** & **Zephaniah 1:12-13** God's people will go through a time when their goods shall become booty; and their houses a desolation; they shall also build houses, but not inhabit them; and they shall plant vineyards, but not drink the wine thereof. This means people will tithe their money and because of wrong teachings, they will not receive any benefits from their tithes (**Deuteronomy 28:38-40; Haggai 1:3-11; Malachi 3:8-10 & Matthew 6:19-20**).

According to these verses, the curses which are in the world have cursed our tithes and caused them to become unbeneficial for us personally. If you haven't caught the revelation: this is depositing our money into our heavenly bank account and not being able to draw from it as yet (**Deuteronomy 28:38-40; Amos 5:11 & Zephaniah 1:12-13**).

In other words, the ministries are getting the benefits of our tithes and offerings and we are NOT receiving any blessings from the tithe. This is because we are not doing the things which allow us to withdraw from our bank account as yet. This is **Deuteronomy 28:28-40; Amos 5:11; Zephaniah 1:12-13; Haggai 1:3-11 & Matthew 6:19** taking place in our lives. This is why we cannot activate our heavenly bank account. The ministries are getting the benefits from our physical money. But the blessings (success, prosperity) we are looking to receive from our giving are still sitting in our heavenly account. And it will not be allowed to be activated until we complete the requirements that it takes to open up our accounts and draw from them.

But, Joel tells us there will come a time when God will restore back to us* what has *been taken. And if we will listen to God and Jesus and do as They instruct us, every penny we have given in God's name will be returned to us with interest.

> **"And I will restore to you the years that the locust hath eaten, the cankerworm, and the caterpillar, and the**

palmerworm, my great army which I sent among you. And ye shall eat in plenty, and be satisfied, and praise the name of the Lord your God, that hath dealt wondrously with you: and my people shall never be ashamed."

Joel 2:25-26

Isaiah 65:21-22 tells us there will come a time when God's people will live in the houses they have built. And they will eat and drink from the gardens and vineyards they have planted. One of the wonderful things about giving our money into God's world is that we never lose what we have given if we follow Jesus' Words and do them (**Deuteronomy 28:1-15; Matthew 7:24-27** & **Luke 6:46-49**).

Whether the curses have eaten the benefits from our tithe or we have just plain lost our money by helping the people with wrong motives; the money we have spent for God's Kingdom is STILL in our account, in heaven (**Matthew 6:20**). No matter how many years go by, the value of our currency is still the same as when we put it in our heavenly account. This is what Jesus meant when He told us no corruption would attack the treasure in heaven.

This means one day we will get a return on our giving and the benefits will be ours, not someone else's, which is what **Joel 2:25-26** & **Isaiah 65:21-22** are saying.

> *"But lay up for yourselves treasures in heaven, where neither moth nor rust doth corrupt, and where thieves do not break through nor steal:"*

Matthew 6:20

You see, I knew the fact which says we need to sow if we want God to bless us (**Galatians 6:7-8** and **Genesis 12:1-3**). But even though I was sowing, there was still no increase in the money as **Joel 2:25-26**; **Isaiah 65:21-22** & **Luke 6:38** were promising.

So, I went to God. There has to be something wrong! Lord, you do not steal from people! You do not want money people need for paying their bills! You are not a cold, heartless God who doesn't care how your people are hurting financially! You do not say to your people, "I do not care if you're hurting or not, you better give me your tithe or you will be in big trouble with Me". What am I doing wrong?

Through a series of teachings from different sources, the Lord gave me the understanding of how to pick out the important information of each series of lessons and put them together. I realize there has not been a full understanding or teaching (1) on Jesus' seed, time, and harvest in Matthew, Mark and Luke; (2) on tithing (**Matthew 6:19-20**); or (3) on God's prosperity (**Deuteronomy 8:18** & **Proverbs 10:22**). Thus, God began to teach me what He wanted me to know on the subject of money, and I would like to pass it on to you.

Please take the time to think about this lesson. God requires us to tithe for our own benefits. The Jewish people have proven this information to be a fact by doing God's laws and tithing. And because they do, God has prospered many of the Jewish people (**Deuteronomy 8:18**).

This is how **Galatians 6:7-8** works in our lives. When we need God, Jesus, and the Holy Spirit's "***Favor***", we must <u>sow</u> into God's Kingdom FIRST, before we can <u>draw on</u> His intervention in our lives (**Galatians 6:7-8; Luke 7:1-5** & **Acts 10:1-4**). We will go into more detail on these facts throughout the book.

CHAPTER 2

No Good "Goods" I

IN THE LAST CHAPTER, we were discussing the fact that, even though the clergy promises the church people will receive some kind of a blessing in return for the offerings given to them, very few people have received the blessings promised. So I went to the Lord and asked Him to show me what was wrong. He gave me His answer by revealing revelation knowledge to me from the scriptures and from some of the different lessons which have been taught throughout the years.

Before we begin, I want you to know whatever is said will be directly from God's Word. As I have said before, my promise to you is to never use my own ideas, opinions or words in this ministry, unless it is to show you how the Holy Spirit used scripture to teach me God and Jesus' Words.

You need to know. Before the Holy Spirit allowed me to share these lessons with you, He guided me and caused me to live through Jesus' Words first. This was so He could have me speak with experience behind the teachings, and NOT just hearsay. Also, this was completed to let YOU know—YOU can do Jesus' Words in the physical, in your life as well as they were done in mine. We can do our Lord's Words because He lived them FIRST and set the way for us to follow in His footsteps (**I Peter 2:21** & **I John 2:6**). Even though these teachings were completed in my life (by using only scripture), I am hoping you will see and understand it is the Holy Spirit speaking to you and not me.

To begin, the Lord showed me, this generation has been sold a bill of No Good "Goods". This fact has to be obvious, because if what the preacher, teacher, pastor, prophet or evangelist has told us was *entirely true*, then the whole church body would be prosperous by now. We can know this is true because, **Deuteronomy 18:17-22** tells us, if what was said by the prophet came from God, then the prophet's words would have come true in our lives within a short time (**Genesis 26:1-12**).

But, if what was said did **_not_** come to pass, then we can know the Lord was NOT completely in the sermon given.

> "**And the Lord said unto me, They have well *spoken* that which they have spoken. I will raise them up a Prophet from among their brethren, like unto thee, *and will put MY WORDS in his mouth*; and he shall speak unto them all that I shall command him. *And it shall come to pass, that whosoever will not hearken unto MY WORDS which he shall speak in my name, I will require it of him.* But the prophet, which shall presume to speak a word in my name, which I have _not_ commanded him to speak, or that shall speak in the name of other gods, even that prophet shall die. And if thou say in thine heart, _How shall we know the word which the Lord hath NOT spoken?_ When a prophet speaketh in the name of the Lord, _if the thing follow not, nor come to pass,_ that *is* the thing which the Lord hath _NOT spoken_, *but* the prophet hath spoken it presumptuously: thou shalt not be afraid of him.**"

> **Deuteronomy 18:17-22**

The Prophet God raised up is *Jesus (Y'shua)*. We know this fact because, we are told, Jesus is the only person who has ever spoken God's Words without making a mistake. Therefore, everything this Prophet said either DID come to pass, or is coming to pass as ongoing events are unfolding before our eyes. There has **never** been a time when Y'shua's Words **have not come to pass.**

However, the bill of No Good "Goods" which was sold to us says: If we want God to be able to bless us as according to **Malachi 3:10, Luke 6:38** & **John 10:10**; the only requirements we must commit to are to believe in Jesus, in and on His name, and to tithe! There are some ministers who also tell us to bless people if we want God to bless us (**Genesis 12:1-3**). And all these things are right. We must be believers in Jesus and in His name and depend on Him and His name! We must also tithe! And we must also bless people if we want God to bless us! But, being told these are the only requirements mandatory in order to be blessed by God cannot be entirely from God.

We can know this is true, because even though many of us have tithed for years, we still have not been blessed in the way we were promised by the Bible. Indeed, some of the clergy have backed off on promising the big blessing. They now only claim that you will be blessed in one way or another.

Again, we can know this teaching is not entirely true either. Because; most of the times, we are not even receiving the little blessings promised. Many times, in spite of the fact we tithe, or sow a seed; our lives remain the same as before we gave our money. Yes, there have been some victories here and there, but it really isn't enough to "write home about".

Deuteronomy 18:21-22 tells us, if the messages taught have not come true in our lives personally, then the lesson was NOT entirely from

God. We are also told in **Genesis 26:1-12,** this miracle can happen in the middle of a famine in a year or less if we will sow in the way God approves.

Deuteronomy 18:21-22 and **Genesis 26:1-12** is how the Lord started revealing to me, the ministers' messages needed God's help. So I asked Him if He would show me what we (as Jesus' Church) needed to do in order to prosper. Then the Holy Spirit started to reveal to me what **Galatians Ch. 3** really means.

According to the clergy of today's churches, the Gentile believers of the New Testament are not required to do the Mosaic Law. **Galatians Ch. 3** is the main scripture used to support this teaching. You need to know, the way the ministers have presented this Chapter to Jesus' people is *grossly wrong.* God, Jesus, and the Holy Spirit are extremely upset with this misunderstanding of **Galatians Ch. 3.**

Why would Paul tell us in **Romans 2:13**, if we *refuse to do* the law, *then Jesus cannot justify us before God?* And on the other hand, tell us in **Galatians Ch. 3** we do NOT have to do the law because we are Gentiles and New Testament believers? This would cause Paul to contradict his "own" words!

> "(For *not* the hearers of the law *are just* before God, *but the doers of the law shall be justified."*

> **Romans 2:13**

This is important for the body of Christ to understand! Doing the law does NOT cause Jesus' people to BECOME JUSTIFIED! When we do perform God's law in our lives, this act only puts us in the position where Jesus *can* justify us (**Matthew 5:17-19 & Hebrews 10:36**). If we **refuse to DO** God's law, then we cannot be put in the position to be *justified* (**Matthew 5:19A** & **Romans 2:13**)! And we NEED to be justified by Jesus if we want to live in heaven (**Matthew 5:20**).

Completing the law is **NOT as impossible** to do as the ministers are always claiming. The law is completed in only ONE commandment.

> "*For **all the law** is fulfilled in one word*, even in this; Thou shalt love thy neighbour as thyself."

> **Galatians 5:14**

> "Therefore all things whatsoever ye would that men should do to you, do ye even so to them: *for this is the law and the prophets*."

> **Matthew 7:12**

> "*A new commandment I give unto you, That ye love one another; as I have loved you, that ye also love one another.*"

> **John 13:34**

> "But Jesus beheld them, and said unto them, With men this is impossible; *but with God all things are possible.*"

> **Matthew 19:26**

> "*For with God nothing shall be impossible.*"

> **Luke 1:37**

According to Jesus' Words in **Matthew 19:26** and Gabriel's words in **Luke 1:37,** if we depend on God to help us fulfill Jesus' commandment in **Matthew 5:19B; 7:12** & **John 13:34** then it is NOT impossible for us to do God's law as explained in **Matthew 7:12** and **Galatians 5:14**.

God tells us in **Joshua 1:8** and Jesus tells us in **Matthew 6:33,** if we will do God's law, then the doing of this law is the thing that will CAUSE the body of Christ to prosper.

> "This book of the law shall not depart out of thy mouth; but thou shalt meditate therein day and night, *that thou mayest observe to do according to all that is written therein:* **for then thou shalt make thy way prosperous, and then thou shalt have good success.**"

> **Joshua 1:8**

> *"But seek ye first the kingdom of God, and his righteousness*; and **all these things shall be added unto you."**

> **Matthew 6:33**

("The all things added to you", IS your prosperity in Jesus' words. And it is the doing of the law that will cause us to prosper in **Joshua 1:8C-E** which is God's Words in Joshua's book).

Since it is the doing of the law which causes us to prosper, and this is true because it is scripture talking to us; then the reverse is also true as well. If you refuse to do God and Jesus' law, you CANNOT prosper!! In other words, do the law you prosper! Don't do the law, you don't prosper! Remember!! It is God who is in control of the money!! And He will be the ONE who will cause you to become rich or poor!

"But thou shalt remember the Lord thy God: *for it is he that giveth thee power to get wealth*, that he may establish his covenant which he sware unto thy father, as it is this day."

Deuteronomy 8:18

The Holy Spirit realizes; it really doesn't seem as though God is in control of the finances because the wicked is rich and the church is basically poor. But God planned the world to be in this condition for His purpose (**James 5:1-7**). (Meditate and allow the Holy Spirit to teach you God's purpose.) This will be explained in our next chapter. But if you do NOT allow the Holy Spirit to deal with you and be open to His teaching, then He will tell you up front, this book will NOT help you!!

CHAPTER 3

No Good "Goods" II

I N OUR LAST CHAPTER the Holy Spirit started to explain God's purpose on allowing the wicked to become rich. But because His lesson would become too long, we closed. He will explain in more detail in this chapter. But again, YOU must be open to the Holy Spirit's teaching and know it is from Him and not me!

Let's return to Jesus' Words in **Matthew 6:33**. In the last chapter, you were told **Matthew 6:33** was the place where Jesus tells us to do God's law. He realizes Y'shua's Words are NOT clear right now. However, if you will read on, you will see how **Matthew 6:33** and **Joshua 1:8** coincide with one another. **Joshua 1:8** tells us to meditate on God's law until we fulfill it in our lives.

Jesus tells us in **Matthew 6:33** to seek God's Kingdom and His righteousness FIRST before we attempt to do anything at all in this world or in God's world as well! What are we doing when we seek God's kingdom? Aren't we studying the Words which will teach us about God's kingdom? This is the only way we can learn or hear about this subject.

"And he said unto them, *I must preach the kingdom of God* to other cities also: for therefore am I sent. And he preached in the synagogues of Galilee."

Luke 4:43-44

Guess what theses Words ARE? They ARE God's law written in the red in the New Testament!! Turn to **Deuteronomy 18:13-22** and read God's Words. He tells us in this scripture, His people do NOT want to hear Him speak any longer. So He will rise up a Prophet who is very MUCH like His people. But this Prophet will teach HIS (God's) WORDS to the people (**John 7:16**).

"Jesus answered them, and said, My doctrine is not mine, but his that sent me."

John 7:16

"And the LORD said unto me, They have well spoken that which they have spoken. I will raise them up a Prophet from among their brethren, like unto thee, and will put my words in his mouth; and he shall speak unto them all that I shall command him."

Deuteronomy 18:17-18

"For I have not spoken of myself; but the Father which sent me, he gave me a commandment, what I should say, and what I should speak. And I know that his commandment is life everlasting: whatsoever I speak therefore, even as the Father said unto me, so I speak."

John 12:49-50

Any time you read Jesus Words which tell you, "The kingdom of heaven is likened unto" Jesus is telling you God's Words which governs (rules) His and God's Kingdom (**Isaiah 7:14-16; 9:6-8; 11:1-5, 11-12; John 1:1-18; 7:16 & 12:49-50**).

Jesus told Pilate in **John 18:36**, His Kingdom is not in this world, but it is in heaven. This fact causes God and Jesus' rules to apply to the Kingdom of Heaven. Because Their rules apply to heaven's domain, this truth allows us the choice of obeying the rules of Their Kingdom or not. If we want to live in God and Jesus' Kingdom, then we are going to have to obey the rules which apply to Their Kingdom because heaven is where they are enforced (**Joel 3:17 & Revelation 21:27**). **Matthew 25:1-12** is one of the rules which apply to Their Kingdom. **Matthew 24:44-51 & Luke 12:37-46** is another rule which applies to this Kingdom.

You need to know, when it comes to the world we are living in, it is your choice whose rules you want to obey (**Romans 6:16**). But when it comes to the world we will live in after death, we MUST obey God and Jesus' rules now, while we are living on this earth, or we will NOT be allowed into heaven (**Matthew 5:17-20 &19:16-21**). We must decide to abide by heaven's rules before we die, or before Jesus returns to this earth to be able to live in the Kingdom Jesus and God controls (**Luke 16:1-13, 15-31 & Revelation 22:14**).

In other words, we are in control and can make a choice of whose rules we want to follow and do while we are living on this earth (**Joshua 24:15 & Romans 6:16**). But in the life we will face after we die, or after Jesus returns to this earth, OUR CHOICE IS GONE! We must submit to Jesus' rules then because He will be in control.

"For unto us a child is born, unto us a son is given: and the government shall be upon his shoulder: . . ."

Isaiah 9: 6A-B

"I have sworn by myself, the word is gone out of my mouth in righteousness, and shall not return, That unto me every knee shall bow, every tongue shall swear."

Isaiah 45:23

This means, Jesus will be in control. And this control causes this fact to become unchangeable (**Philippians 2:9-11**). Consequently, Jesus will be the One who will choose our final destination. Therefore, we must decide to follow His rules now, or suffer the consequences of not doing so (**John 12:48** & **Acts 3:23**).

Jesus will return to judge us as according to the rules we have chosen to follow. There is too much scripture to copy, but if you will turn to **Matthew 25:31-46** and read Jesus' Words with an open heart, you will see what He is telling us. If we have chosen to listen, follow and obey His Words while we are living on this earth, then our Lord will judge us according to His rules which we have chosen to follow and allow us to live with Him (**Matthew 19:16-21; 25:31-40; Mark 10:17-21; Luke 18:18-22; John 10:1-5** & **12:48**).

But if we have chosen to listen, follow and obey the false prophet's words, then we are in big trouble (**Matthew 25:41-46**). We will be judged by the words we chose to follow and complete in our lives (**Deuteronomy 18:17-22; Isaiah 45:23; John 12:48: Acts 3:23** & **Philippians 2:9-11**).

Remember, it is Jesus and God who applies the rules to their Kingdom, not Satan, and not us! Therefore, They are the Ones who will allow us through the gates and to be able to stay there once we are in (**Matthew 8:10-12**). Or They are the Ones who throw us out of Their Kingdom if we are there illegally (**Matthew 22:1-14**). After all, *it is Their Kingdom*. God made it, He and Jesus rules it. And if we want to live in it, then we must abide by their rules, not OURS!!

> "And it shall come to pass, that every soul, which will not hear that prophet, shall be destroyed from among the people".

> **Acts 3:23**

Thus when we are told to seek God's Kingdom in **Matthew 6:33**, we are being told to seek the Words which teach us the rules of His and God's Kingdom (**Isaiah 9:6; Luke 4:43-44; John 3:3-5 & 12:48-50**)!! Doesn't Jesus tell us in **John 12:48**, if we reject His Words, then we will be ruled and judged by the very Words we rejected?

> "He that, rejecteth me, and receiveth not my words, hath one that judgeth him: the word that I have spoken, the same shall judge him in the last day."

> **John 12:48**

This judgment causes Jesus' Words which are God's Words to become the law which will rule and regulate us when it comes time for us to enter into God and Jesus' Kingdom.

"For I have not spoken of myself; but the Father which sent me, he gave me a commandment, what I should say, and what I should speak."

John 12:49

And if we refuse to obey and complete this law in our lives before we die, or before Jesus returns to this earth, we cannot get into God's Kingdom because we are rejecting Jesus' Words. He told us in **John 3:1-5**, we must be born again before we are allowed to enter into His Kingdom.

"Jesus answered, Verily, verily, I say unto thee, ***Except a man be born*** of water ***and of the Spirit,*** he cannot enter into the kingdom of God."

John 3:5

Remember, it is Jesus' Words which are the Spirit of God.

"It is the spirit that quickeneth; the flesh profiteth nothing: *the words that I speak unto you,* ***they are spirit,*** and they are life."

John 6:63

We must be born of these Words before we are allowed to enter God's Kingdom (**John 3:5**). How are we born of Jesus' Words which are God's Words (**John 7:16; 12:49-50; & 14:10, 24**); which are the Spirit we must be born of (**John 3:5**)? By doing God's Will.

"He came unto his own, and his own received him not. But as many as received him, to them gave he power to become the sons of God, even to them that believe on his name: _**Which were born**_ not of blood, nor of the will of the flesh, nor of the _**will**_ of man, _**but of God.**_"

John 1:11-13

"Not every one that saith unto me, Lord, Lord, shall enter into the kingdom of heaven; _**but he that doeth the will of my Father**_ _which is in heaven._"

Matthew 7:21

You do the will of God by doing Jesus' Words (**John 6:40, 53-54, 56 & I John 3:24**). This will be explained in detail later on in the book. Jesus' Words are the SAME commandments (rules) as God's Words (**John 8:28**). God's Words are the law of God (**Deuteronomy 27:9-10**). Therefore, according to Jesus' teachings in **Matthew 6:33; Luke 4:43-44; John 7:16;12:48-50; 3:5; 6:63;1:11-13; Matthew 7:21; John 6:40,53-54, 56; I John 3:24; John 8:28 & Deuteronomy 27:9-10** we are to seek God's law and do it before the "all things" will be added to us!!

Jesus tells us to seek these Words. If we obey this command, we will end up meditating on God's law!! Once we meditate on Jesus' Words, they will become a part of our makeup, because you cannot ponder and separate from the Words you are meditating on.

"For as he thinketh in his heart, so is he: . . ."

Proverbs 23:7A

Once the law becomes a part of your makeup, you do complete it in your life! Doesn't **Joshua 1:8** tell us, if we will meditate on God's law day and night, we WILL do it!

> "This book of the law shall not depart out of thy mouth; but thou shalt meditate therein day and night, that thou mayest observe to do according to all that is written therein: for then thou shalt make thy way prosperous, and then thou shalt have good success."

Joshua 1:8

If we *refuse* to do God's law referred to in **Joshua 1:8** and **Matthew 6:33**, then there is NO WAY Jesus' Church will ever prosper. Because according to Jesus' Words in **Matthew 5:19A** the people who *refuse* to do God's law are the least in God's Kingdom. The least people become the last on the list to receive help from God (**Deuteronomy 28:43-48, Matthew 5:19A; 7:26-27; Luke 6:49 & 16:1-13**).

This is why the wicked have prospered. They have robbed, stepped on, and violently taken the church's prosperity (**Amos 5:11; Zephaniah 1:12-13 Deuteronomy 28:38-40; Psalm 73:1-6; Ecclesiastes Ch. 11; Haggai 1:6**). They have been allowed to receive the church's success, because we as the church body, have NOT completed the requirements (God's law) which will cause us to retain our wealth (**Joshua 1:8 & Matthew 6:33**). Remember, if we chose to not do the law, then we cannot be justified (**Romans 2:13**). If we cannot be justified, then we cannot prosper (**Proverbs 28:13**). If we cannot retain the prosperity (success) of the world, the only other place for the riches to live, is with the wicked (**Ecclesiastes 6:1-2**).

Thus, in the rest of this book, the Holy Spirit will teach you how you can DO God's law so you can prosper!! This can happen if, and only if, you will listen, take Jesus' Words to heart and do them from the inside out.

Again, just so you know, the bill of No Good "Goods" which has been sown into the Christian world says this: There is no responsibility on our end of our agreement between God and ourselves except (1) to accept Jesus into our hearts; (2) to make sure we believe Jesus is God's Son; (3) to make sure we believe He died for us on the cross; (4) to make sure we believe in and on Jesus' name and (5) to **_tithe_** to the church. In other words, make sure we support the ministries.

Yes, the ministers are right in telling us to support them. What we sow **_we will reap_**. Therefore, if we refuse to sow money into God's Kingdom by refusing to help the people who stand for God, then there is **_no money in our heavenly bank account_** for us to reap. Thus, when it comes time for God to transfer the money from the sinner to the just, we will not have any money in our heavenly account to reap!

> "Lay not up for yourselves treasures upon earth, where moth and rust doth corrupt, and where thieves break through and steal: But lay up for yourselves treasures in heaven, where neither moth nor rust doth corrupt, and where thieves do not break through nor steal:"

> **Matthew 6:19-20**

But be warned: make sure you support the ministries God and Jesus approve of. You could sow your money into a wrong teaching, and then you will not receive any benefit from your sowing any more than you have in the past (**Amos 5:11** & **Zephaniah 1:12-13**).

"Give not that which is holy unto the dogs, neither cast ye your pearls before swine, lest they trample them under their feet, and turn again and rend you."

Matthew 7:6

It is not that you will not eventually get a return on your money given to God. You will if you obey Jesus' commandments (**Joel 2:25-26 & Isaiah 65:21-22**). It is that you will not receive your benefit when you do the sowing because **Matthew 7:6** will take place in your life. Jesus' Words are true and they will happen. Sadly it is only the negative Words which happen first. This is because we must learn the positive Words and do them before they will be fulfilled in our lives.

If you don't obey Jesus' Words, then there is no hope for any of your money you have given to God. Sorry this is just the way Jesus' teachings have been set in the scriptures (**Proverb 13:22; Matthew 5:17-19 & Romans 2:13**).

Because **Proverbs 13:22; Matthew 5:17-19 & Romans 2:13** are true, if you knowingly give your money to a wrong teaching, Jesus' Words in **Matthew 7:6** will come true in your life. The ministry will use your money for their purpose. And for now, your benefits will go out of the window (**Micah 6:15-16**).

Just make sure you pray before you give. Search for the agreement which comes from the Holy Spirit who dwells on the inside of your body. The God-given Spirit which lives on the inside of you will agree with what is being said if it is right with God.

"But he that is spiritual judgeth all things, yet he himself is judged of no man. For who hath known the mind of the Lord, that he may instruct him? But we have the mind of Christ."

I Corinthians 2:15-16

"Henceforth I call you not servants; for the servant knoweth not what his lord doeth: but I have called you friends; for all things that I have heard of my Father I have made known unto you."

John 15:15

Believing in and on Jesus and tithing is NOT the ONLY responsibility we have to perform in our lives, if we want God to prosper us. We MUST DO the law as well (**Joshua 1:8** & **Matthew 5:17-19**). Therefore, the Holy Spirit will begin to show you how to complete God's law in your lives in our next chapter.

(This is just a note. I wouldn't be qualified to write this book if the Holy Spirit hadn't caused me to live through Jesus' commandments before sharing them with you. He has. Therefore He can and does tell me what to write and I do write it) (**John 14:26; 16:12-15**).

Requirements for Success

H I AND WELCOME BACK! If you have returned, this means you are interested enough to move on with Jesus. Good for you! God and Jesus are very PROUD of you for having enough interest on the inside of yourself to travel on with Them **(Isaiah 49:15-16).**

The Holy Spirit realizes that what was said in Chapter 2 and 3 is _not_ popular and almost unheard of in this day and age. But, it is the truth from God and Jesus' Kingdom **(Deuteronomy 18:18-19; Joshua 1:8; Proverbs 13:22; Matthew 5:17-19; 6:33 Luke 6:38; John 10:10 & Romans 2:13).** Consequently, if we want to prosper and _remain successful for the rest of our lives_, then we cannot ignore God's law **(Matthew 6:33; Joshua 1:8 & James 5:1-6).**

There are people who are NOT interested in God's prosperity as long as they have enough money to live comfortably. However, they **are** interested in living in heaven. And/or they **do** want the promises in the Bible, but when it comes to God's prosperity, they just don't think about it.

For example, there are Christians who have lost their health. There are believers who cannot seem to get along with their spouses and other people at work or at home. Many Christians are having trouble with their children. There are Christians who are looking for good employment. There are believers who are being abused. There are single men and women who want to get married, but can't seem to find a good spouse. Others are married, but don't have good marriages. Christians have lost their homes. And the list could go on and on. Jesus wants you to know, the same rules which apply to becoming prosperous, apply to being able to receive your promises from God. As was said in the last lesson, if you refuse to do God's law, you are considered by God and Jesus as being the least in God's Kingdom.

> "Whosoever therefore shall break one of these least commandments, and shall teach men so, he shall be called the least in the kingdom of heaven: . . ."

Matthew 5:19A

Therefore, if you continue to refuse to do God's law, you will be deemed as being the least. The least (the last one on the list) becomes one of the last ones in line whose requests' is considered. This is the way it is in this world. This is also the way it works in heaven, as well (**Matthew 5:19A**).

As a result, if you are **not** interested in God's prosperity, this is fine with God and Jesus. But, if you refuse to do God's law because you don't want the prosperity, then this refusal of doing the law is going to cause you to lose your answers to your prayers (**John 15:16**). This is why people pray, but when they do, they feel as if their prayers don't reach any higher then their ceilings.

You must realize, because of Satan, God honors His Words in **Isaiah 57:16-17; 59:1-3 & John 9:31** more than He honors a person who is allowing his/her sin to control their life (**James 4:1-3**). This is why Jesus forgave the man who was sick of the palsy first, before He healed the man in **Matthew 9:1-2; Mark 2:1-11 & Luke 5:17-24**. You must be able to be justified by Jesus (**Romans 2:13**) before God can begin to answer your prayers in the way you want Him to answer you (**Isaiah 59:1-3; Matthew 9:1-2; Mark 2:1-11 & Luke 5:17-24**). Consequently, let's study the law.

Since **Matthew 6:33** and **Joshua 1:8** is the same commandment, and most born-again Christians only live their lives from the New Testament, we are going to study the Words quoted in **Joshua 1:8** from Jesus' Words in **Matthew 6:33**. Let's get started, shall we?

The very first thing Jesus requires from us, as His people, is to study His Words until they become a part of our lives. Doesn't He tell us in **Matthew 6:33** to seek God's Kingdom *first* before anything can be added unto us from God's world and/or from the physical world?

> *"But seek ye **first** the kingdom of God, and his righteousness; and all these things shall be added unto you."*

Matthew 6:33

Most people read **Matthew 6:33** and apply them as if Jesus said "all things will be added to us <u>while we are seeking the physical world and God's Kingdom at the same time.</u>" Read Jesus' Words closely. He tells His people to seek God's Kingdom first. After we have sought for ourselves God's Kingdom and have gotten His Kingdom into our blood, *then*, and only then, will God start adding the things from the world to us. So we could read Jesus' words in the way He said them like this: 'But seek ye first the Kingdom of God and His righteousness and (*then* <u>after we have gotten His Kingdom down on the inside of our bodies and blood</u>), *then* all these things shall be added unto us.'

We know this is the way Jesus is saying these words because in **Matthew 6:24** He has already told us we *cannot serve two masters at the same time.* We cannot seek and/or serve in God's Kingdom while seeking the things of the world at the same time.

> *"No man can serve two masters: for either he will hate the one, and love the other; or else he will hold to the one, and despise the other. Ye cannot serve God and mammon."*

Matthew 6:24

In other words, we cannot seek God's Kingdom while our attention is on the world at the *same time*. We must use our minds to concentrate on God's Kingdom *only*. This means; we must get to the place in our minds where we can relate everything to God's truths.

For example: in our minds, we are preoccupied on the Bible lesson we studied the night before, in place of the world's things. This means, instead of letting our minds be on the world's affairs (on the job we are doing at work; the story we just read in the paper; the television program that interested us; the computer program we are working on; or the movie we just watched), our minds would be studying God's Word. In our minds, we would be thinking of ways to apply the Bible lesson we just studied. This is one of the ways we are to use our minds to meditate on God's law, and to seek God's Kingdom as well (**Joshua 1:8A** & **Matthew 6:33**).

Just because **Joshua 1:8A** tells us to meditate on the law of God day and night; God is not telling you to use your time at work for God's study time. You are required to give your employer an honest day's work. But this commandment does mean that your leisure time should be used on studying God's law (**II Timothy 2:15**). Your job, the newspaper, the television, the computer, the movies or movie stars are NOT foremost in your mind any longer because, God and Jesus' Words have replaced those items.

Remember? Jesus' Words tell us about God's Kingdom (**Luke 4:43**). We are required to meditate on Jesus' Words if we want God's help (**Joshua 1:8** & **Matthew 6:33**). When we obey this command and do meditate on the words of Y'shua, this act causes us to seek God's Kingdom (**Matthew 6:33**). While we are seeking God's Kingdom, we are meditating on God's law at the same time because Jesus' Words and God's law are one in the same (**Deuteronomy 18:18** & **John 8:28**).

Again, Remember? Jesus' Words are the law of God being fulfilled in the New Testament (**Matthew 5:17-18**). Hence, when we are studying these Words, we are studying the way God's law is to be fulfilled in our lives (**I Peter 2:21** & **I John 2:6**). Now, let's read how we are to put Jesus' command in **Matthew 6:33** into action and see how Jesus and God's Words coincide one with the other.

The first part of **Joshua 1:8** tells us to meditate on God's law day and night.

> "This book of the law shall not depart out of thy mouth; but thou shalt meditate here in day and night, . . ."

Joshua 1:8A-B

The first part of Jesus' commandment in **Matthew 6:33** tells us to seek God's Kingdom. This is the very same commandment God tells us to do in **Joshua 1:8A-B**. We are to meditate (seek) God's law (God's Kingdom) day and night.

"Why are we told to meditate on (seek) God's law (God's Kingdom) day and night? "... that thou mayest observe to do according to all that is written therein: ..."

Joshua 1:8C

So this Kingdom becomes such a part of our lives that we will just end up doing Jesus' Words automatically. You see, what you think about most of the time, is what you end up doing in the physical.

"For as he thinketh in his heart, so is he: ..."

Proverbs 23:7A

The proof that **Proverbs 23:7A** is true are serial killers. They strategically make their plans in their minds, before they make their moves on their victims. This is how they cause their plans to work and create problems for the police to solve their crimes. This is called meditating on the wrong things. But, it does work for a while. The wheels of justice grind slow, but they do grind and eventually the crime doesn't pay (**Ecclesiastes 8:5-8** & **II Peter 2:9**).

In like manner, if we will meditate on Jesus' Words in the same way or as much as the serial killers meditate on their murders, we will end up doing Jesus' Words just as the assassins end up doing their felonies.

Only we will be well rewarded for doing God's law and we will NOT end our lives hurting as you will see in our next few sentences ((**Matthew 5:12** & **Galatians 5:22-23**). You see — God's Words work. They either work for the good, or the bad. It is up to you to decide how you want to use **Proverbs 23:7A.**

Subsequently, if we will meditate on God's law, then we WILL end up doing His law in our lives (**Joshua 1:8A-C**).

Why would we want to do God's law?

> ". . . for then thou shalt make thy way prosperous, and then thou shalt have good success."

Joshua 1:8D

Doing God's law will cause us to become prosperous and successful. This means doing the law will cause us to be able to receive answered prayers in the way that will make us successful (**John 15:16**). So now, we can acquire our health (**Matthew 13:15**). Doing the law causes us to grow in God (**Matthew 12:33**). As we mature, we become strong enough to stop allowing others to abuse us (**Luke 10:19**). Our Lord can now bless us with better employment (**Psalm 37:25 & John 15:16**). Doing the law will cause us to become better people; therefore, we can have better relationships with one another and find good spouses (**I John 1:7**). Are you beginning to know why it is important we DO God's law in our lives? This is the way it works.

> "This book of the law shall not depart out of thy mouth; but thou shalt meditate therein day and night,"

Joshua 1:8A

> "But seek ye first the kingdom of God, and his righteousness; . . ."

Matthew 6:33A

Meditate on the Words which tell you about God's Kingdom. In other words, meditate on God's law (**Joshua 1:8A** & **Matthew 6:33A)**. The Words of God's Kingdom, (the law) will get down into the depth of your mind and your heart, as you meditate. Once you get God and Jesus' Words down on the inside of your heart, *you will want to do what you have concentrated on*.

"For as he thinketh in his heart, so is he: . . ."

Proverbs 23:7

After you start to do what you have meditated on from the Bible lesson, the doing of God's Words, and the continuing to do the law will set you in line so you can begin to prosper. And it will begin to set God free to be able to start answering your prayers (**Joshua 1:8**; **Matthew 6:33** & **John 15:16)**.

Notice Jesus did **not** say our minds would stay like this forever. He said to seek God's Kingdom **first,** and then the world's things shall be added to us. We cannot walk around with our heads in the clouds all our lives. Have you ever heard the words which say, "She is so heavenly minded she is no earthly good?"

We live in this world. We have to function with other people. Therefore, the things of the world will be added back to us after we have gotten Jesus' Words rooted down into our bodies.

We only constantly meditate day and night, without the things of the world, until God's Kingdom gets *rooted* down on the inside of our bodies. And, we want to do the words of the law from the inside out. Once this act happens, God's law (Jesus' Words) just becomes a part of our lives forever. Thus, even though we do the things of the world, we will always have God's Kingdom in the back of our minds.

Consequently, we will react in the world as according to God's law. We need Jesus' Words rooted into our hearts so we can remain successful in our lives (**James 5:1-7**).

Remember, Jesus tells us in **Matthew 13:21** because we do not have any root down on the inside of our bodies, we become offended. And because we become offended we become unsuccessful in our lives (**Matthew 13:21-22**).

Therefore, again, the first and foremost commandment is to meditate on Jesus' Words so they will become rooted down into our hearts (**Matthew 6:33; 13:18-21 & Joshua 1:8**). Once we meditate, we will want to do what is foremost in our minds. This is why **Proverbs 23:7** tells us we will do in the physical what we think about in our minds.

"For as he thinketh in his heart, so is he: . . ."

Proverbs 23:7

Because this chapter is getting long, the Holy Spirit cannot finish teaching all that goes with meditation in this chapter, so we will close for now and pick up the rest of the details in our next lesson.

CHAPTER 5

Meditation I

IN THIS CHAPTER WE will pick up where we left off in our last session. Remember? The first thing we are told to do in **Joshua 1:8** and in **Matthew 6:33;** is to meditate. There are several reasons why Jesus requires us to ponder His Words. We will cover nine of them in this lesson.

The first reason to meditate is to seek God's Kingdom (**Matthew 6:33**). This is important because, we are NOT allowed to receive any help from God unless we SEEK His Kingdom FIRST. Remember? Jesus told us in our last lesson it is only after we have sought God's Kingdom for ourselves, then, and ONLY THEN will all things be added to us.

> "But seek ye FIRST the kingdom of God, and his righteousness; and all these things shall be added unto you."

> **Matthew 6:33**

The second reason we are called to meditate on God's Kingdom is to cause us to study. One of the ways to seek God's Kingdom is to do a personal Bible study (**Proverbs 2:1-6**; & **II Timothy 2:14-15**).

We learn to study by first, picking one of God's promises which has a personal meaning to us. It could be we want our health (**Matthew 13:15**). It could be we want a good marriage (**Matthew 19:3-12**). It could be we want God's acceptance (**Matthew 19:16-21**). The list could go on and on, but we would take this whole chapter just putting down the different promises we want.

The point is; pick the promise from God's Word which means the most to you. Find scripture that applies to your situation and do a personal Bible study on the verses. It would be good if you took a big concordance and looked up all the scriptures which pertain to the promise you are studying (**Proverbs 2:1-11** & **Matthew 6:33**). I personally use "Strong's Exhaustive Concordance Of The Bible". But you can use any one which suits you. But do use one of them.

(For example, let's say you are looking for God's acceptance. Take the concordance and look up the word accept, acceptable, acceptably, acceptance, acceptation, accepted, acceptest, accepteth, accepting, worth, worthless, worthily, worthy, approve, approved, approvest, approveth, approving and all the rest of the words which deal with your acceptance by God. Then take the Bible and look up and read all the references which the concordance shows you. Write in a notebook the promises which talk to YOU personally. As you are studying the verses, there will be footnotes within the scriptures you are reading. Look up the footnotes as well. Write in a notebook the promises which uplift YOU personally *and recite* them to yourself every morning.

Read Jesus' commandments as if they are written to YOU PERSONALLY and not necessarily to the ones in the scriptures. Remember! The Bible was left on this earth so the Words written in it could become your own personal orders.

If you will listen to these commandments as if they were written to YOU ONLY and DO what they say to do, the Bible Words will lead you to YOUR heavenly Father. Do NOT read Jesus' commandments (Words) as if they were written to the people in the Bible. They were, but they were also written to YOU PERSONALLY. And if you will start to read ALL the scriptures in this fashion, this study will open up a whole new avenue of understanding for you.

You are NOT allowed to just pick the good scriptures out of the Bible and say these are the only verses written to ME personally. If you are going to stand and believe the good promises, then you are going to have to read and receive the Words which teach you how to mature as well. This is the ONLY way you will win God's approval of you (**Matthew 12:33-37**). As you study these scriptures you will find out **Matthew 8:5-10; 10:38; 19:16-21; Luke 7:1-7; Acts Ch. 10** are only a few verses which tell you this fact.

If we do this kind of seeking, it will allow us to start to understand the scriptures from God and Jesus' viewpoint (**Isaiah 55:7-11; Matthew 6:33 & 11:28-30**).

The third reason our heavenly Father and Y'shua want us to meditate on Their Words is to gain Their understanding of the scriptures (**Matthew 13:10-19; 16:13-18; Romans 12:2; Ephesians 4:20-24; & Colossians 3:10**). This understanding is Their pathway to our victory over life (**Matthew 13:10-19 & 16:13-19**). Once we start accepting the scriptures from God and Jesus' perspective, then we will be granted the knowledge to know how to divide (use) the Word in the RIGHT way (**II Timothy 2:15B**).

The fourth reason to study and meditate on God and Jesus' Words is to gain God's approval of our lives. If we will settle down and truly start to study to the point in which we can receive God's revealed knowledge from God and Jesus' viewpoint of the Bible, then God will approve of us (**II Timothy 2:14-15** & **Matthew 16:13-19**).

Our fifth reason to meditate on God's Words is to change the way we think. When we start to comprehend God, Jesus and the Holy Spirit's understanding of the scriptures, this understanding will cause us to change our thinking from the world's attitude of life into God and Jesus' interpretations of life (**Isaiah 55:7-11**; & **Ephesians 4:21-24**).

The sixth reason to meditate on God's Words is to be able to receive our own personal revelation knowledge from God (**Matthew 16:17-19**). You cannot receive God's revealed knowledge until you start to gain the comprehension of God, Jesus and the Holy Spirit's understanding of the scriptures (**Matthew 13:15** & **Isaiah 55:7-11**).

The seventh reason to meditate is so that Satan cannot rob God's promises from you (**Matthew 13:11-19; Mark 4:14-15;** & **Luke 8:11-12**). Jesus tells us in **Matthew 16:12-18** it is only revelation knowledge which the gates of hell cannot prevail against!! Thus, unless you study to be able to gain God's revealed knowledge on your promise, the gates of hell can and DO prevail against you. Consequently, because you do NOT know and understand God and Jesus' promises from God's revelation knowledge (God's perspective), Satan has the RIGHT and does rob your promises from you (**Matthew 13:18-19**).

The eighth reason to meditate is to cause God's promises and Jesus' Words to become rooted down into the depths of our souls. Once our promise becomes rooted, it doesn't matter who offends us, we will remember our promise. And this promise will become MORE important to us then the offense (**Matthew 13:23; Mark 4:20;** & **Luke 8:15**). This reason will be explained in a further chapter.

And the ninth reason to meditate is to be able to gain our VICTORY over life (**Matthew 16:12-19** & **John 10:10**).

All of us are going to encounter problems in our lives. The answers to our problems are in the Bible! The first thing Jesus tells us, is to seek for the answers to our problems in His Words (**Matthew 6:25-33** & **7:7-8**). His Words are our seeds which enter into our mind(s) by reading and hearing the scriptures (**Matthew 13:18-19; Mark 4:14-15** & **Luke 8:11-12**).

Since the explanation of these scriptures is long, and this chapter is longer than originally planned, let the Holy Spirit explain this fact in His next lesson.

CHAPTER 6

Meditation II

THE HOLY SPIRIT CLOSED the last chapter by giving us **Matthew 13:18-19; Mark 4:14-15** and **Luke 8:11-12** to read. He had said, "God's promises are our seeds which enter into our mind(s) by reading the scriptures. This fact needs to be explained. He intends to complete His Words in this chapter.

We are told by Jesus in **Matthew 13:18**; in **Mark 4:14**; and in **Luke 8:11** God's Word is our seed. Our seeds, (God's Words), are sown into our mind(s) by God and Jesus' Words written in the Old and New Testaments. Thus, it is our seed (God's promises) which will give us our way out from under our troubles.

For example: let's say you are having financial problems in your life. Then God's promise for you is in **Proverbs 13:22; Luke 6:38; John 10:10;** and in **James 5:1-8**. Let's say you are married, but you are having marital problems. God's promise for you is in **Genesis 2:24** and in **Matthew 19:4-9**. Let's say you are having problems with your children. God's promise for you is in **Isaiah 54:13; Matthew 15:4; Mark 7:10** and in **Ephesians 6:1-4**. Let's say your health is failing. God's promise for you is in **Proverbs 3:1-8; Isaiah 53:5** and in **Matthew 13:15**. Need good employment? God's promise for you is in **Psalm 37:25** and in **Matthew 6:24-34**. What if you are being abused? God's promise for you is in **Psalm 81:13-14; Proverbs 16:7** and in **Matthew 13:15**. Once you learn God's ways and DO His ways in your life, God promises to subdue your enemies and turn His hand against your adversaries in **Psalm 81:13-14**. He also promises you peace with your enemies in **Proverbs 16:7**. Or let's say that you are single and want a mate. God's promise for you is in **Matthew 7:12, 17-19; John 15:16** and in **Galatians 5:22-23**. Everyone is attracted to a person who is kind and genuinely gives the fruits of the Spirit from the inside out.

All of the above are just some of God and Jesus' answers to a few of the church's problems. If these problems apply to you personally, and you have taken the time to look up the scriptures and read the Words written, you have found your answers from the different books of the Bible. The answer to your own personal problem is now sown in your mind (**Matthew 13:18-19A; Mark 4:14-15A; & Luke 8:11-12A**). And you probably feel as if you can stand on your Bible promise forever!

However, if you refuse to do the personal Bible study and meditate on your new found knowledge, your promise for your problem is still just in your mind only. And as long as it just sits in your consciousness, your guarantee CANNOT help you overcome your trouble.

This is how it works. Let's say you need good health. Jesus promises to heal you in **Proverbs 3:1-8; Isaiah 53:5** and **Matthew 13:15**. You find these scriptures in the Bible and read them for yourself. This is the process of receiving your promise of "good health" from God and Jesus. This is **Matthew 13:18, 20; Mark 4:14, 16 & Luke 8:11, 13** taking place in your life.

Since you have read your assurance, your guarantee of this promise is in your mind. This is **Matthew 13:19; Mark 4:15 & Luke 8:12** taking place in your life. If you have NOT meditated on your seed, your promise will not move from your mind down into the depths of your heart. This is **Matthew 13:18-21A; Mark 4:14-17A & Luke 8:11-13A-B** taking place in your life. Thus, you have **not** caused your seed to become rooted on the inside of you. This is **Matthew 13:21; Mark 4:17 & Luke 8:13B** taking place in your life. And your answer is still just in your mind only!

The Holy Spirit cannot emphasize the importance of meditating enough! Because, when the hard pain from your sickness attacks you, there are no Words from the depths of your soul which will rise up to your mind so you can combat the pain. Remember: they are still just in your head. Let the Holy Spirit explain.

Your head cannot concentrate on two things at the same time. Therefore, when the pain from your sickness attacks your body, your mind will STOP thinking about your seed and will focus in on your throbbing! This is when Satan removes your promise from your mind (**Matthew 13:19; Mark 4:15 & Luke 8:12**). You will forget anything at all about any kind of scripture, because you will be concentrating on your pain. Again, this is **Matthew 13:19; Mark 4:15 & Luke 8:12** taking place in your life.

Because your seed (your promise) is not in your mind any longer your Bible promise has left your body (**Matthew 13:19**). Remember, because you didn't study, your promise didn't move from your mind into your God-given Spirit. And when your promise left your mind there was nothing left. This is because there was no root (or Words from your Bible promise) on the inside of your God-given Spirit. This root (or Words) would have risen from your Spirit up into your mind to help you fight off the pain. But, because you didn't study, the Words were not in your Spirit to help you fight.

Hence, your pain will remain in your body and you will be attacked by your sickness over and over again. Because there isn't any seed (or Bible Words) to fight your disease, you are left with your sickness (**Matthew 13:18-21**). And God's promise will NOT be able to help you! This is just one example of how life works without God's promises becoming rooted on the inside of you.

What was true for sickness is also true for every other problem people encounter. **Matthew 13:21; Mark 4:17** and **Luke 8:13** applies to every trial known to mankind.

Remember: **Isaiah 5:13** and **Hosea 4:6** tell us we WILL be destroyed if we do NOT know the scriptures from God's revelation knowledge. It is only our Heavenly Father's revealed knowledge which the gates of hell CANNOT penetrate against.

> "And Jesus answered and said unto him, *Blessed art thou Simon Barjona:* **for flesh and blood hath not revealed it unto thee, but my Father which is in heaven.** *And I say also unto thee, That thou art Peter, and* **upon this rock I will build my church; and the gates of hell shall not prevail against it.**"

> **Matthew 16:17-18**

God is always trying to give us His revealed knowledge (**Matthew 13:10-14**)! But, it is not until we come down off of our own "pride" and open up our minds to our Creator and Jesus' perception of the scriptures that we can begin to receive our LORD'S revelation knowledge.

> "Let the wicked forsake his way and the unrighteous man his thoughts; and let him return unto the LORD, and he

will have mercy upon him; and to our God, for he will abundantly pardon. For my thoughts are not your thoughts, neither are your ways my ways, saith the LORD. For as the heavens are higher than the earth, so are my ways higher than your ways, and my thoughts than your thoughts."

Isaiah 55:7-9

"For this people's heart is waxed gross, and their ears are dull of hearing, and their eyes they have closed; lest at any time they should see with their eyes, and hear with their ears, and should understand with their heart, and should be converted, and I should heal them."

Matthew 13:15

"If so be that ye have heard him, and have been taught by him, as the truth is in Jesus: That ye put off concerning the former conversation the old man, which is corrupt according to the deceitful lusts; And be renewed in the spirit of your mind; And that ye put on the NEW MAN, which after God is created in righteousness and true holiness."

Ephesians 4:21-24

We only receive this knowledge through meditation (**Matthew 13:10-19**)! And without the revealed knowledge, Satan takes our promise when we need it the most (**Matthew 13:19-21; Mark 4:15-17 & Luke 8:12-13**).

But when we do meditate and we do produce root on the inside of our Spirits by receiving God's knowledge, then Satan cannot steal our promise from us (**Matthew 16:18**). So this can be understood, let's look at another example of how Jesus' parable of the sower works.

Let's say you are the person who needs good employment. You look **Psalm 37:25** up in the scriptures and you read your promise and believe it was written for you personally.

> "I have been young, and now am old; yet have I not seen the righteous forsaken, nor his seed begging bread."

Psalm 37:25

You are the one who has taken Jesus' Words seriously, so you take your concordance and look up all the scriptures which apply to the words forsaken, begging, and bread. As you are reading, studying and writing, God's promise becomes rooted down into your heart. Therefore, the opposite of **Matthew 13:21A** starts to take place in your heart and you believe beyond a shadow of a doubt that God's people will not have to beg for food.

You are impressed to look in the help wanted ads and happen to see a position which suits your qualifications and you apply. You are called for an interview. When you stand before your interviewer you notice how many other applications are laying on his/her desk. This makes you nervous and you are not sure how the meeting is going. You really need this job. All of a sudden your Bible promise enters your mind, and you quote it in your mind. You see, when you are standing in front of your interviewer, you are not thinking about scripture anymore than the sick person was thinking about his promise when he was in pain.

The difference was the meditation. Through meditating, the person who needed the job had scripture in his/her heart. When the persecuting, the affliction was taking place, even though the scripture verse was not in the person's mind it was in his/her heart. And when it was needed the most, God could come through for the person. Our Lord had scripture to work with. He had the person's God-given Spirit send the verse from his/her heart into their head. This couldn't happen for the sick person because there was no written Word in the man's/woman's heart to send to the person's mind. Let's return to the rest of the trial for the job hunter.

Of course, the person was told; if he/she was wanted, the interviewer will let him/her know. The person's thoughts would be, "Did his/her efforts with God work"?

What do the scriptures say? Stay single minded (**James 1:1-8**). Do not let the persecutor (Satan) rob you of your promise. Do not let **Matthew 13:19-21; Mark 4:15-17** & **Luke 8:12-13** take place in your life. Just keep quoting your seed (**Psalm 37:25**). Write it again and again if this is what it takes to be able to sustain the scripture and stay away from the doubt. Realize, you are being tested to see how faithful you will remain to God, Jesus and your promise.

Remember Jairus? He was tested just as much. When he was told his daughter was dead, Jesus told Jairus:

> "But when Jesus heard it, he answered him, saying, *Fear not: believe only, and she shall be made whole.*"

> **Luke 8:50**

You are to exercise the SAME kind of faith in **Psalm 37:25** as Jairus did in Jesus' Words. And guess what? *You will get a call.*

"For his anger endureth, but a moment; in his favour is life: weeping may endure for a night, but joy cometh in the morning."

Psalms 30:5

"But that on the good ground are they, which in an honest and good heart, having heard the word, **keep it, _and bring forth fruit with patience_**."

Luke 8:15

We NEED our promises rooted. Because: unless our guarantees are ingrained on the inside of us, we will not have enough strength to fight off the trials which will attack our lives (**Matthew 13:18-21**). Remember Jesus' trial in the wilderness? It was only the written Word which backed Satan out of Jesus' life (**Matthew 4:1-11** & **Luke 4:1-13**).

Let's look at this truth from a different angle. Let's say you are the person who is having marital problems. Your husband fooled you by saying he was a Christian and he did all the things which proved this information to you, until you married him. Now he is abusing you. Neither does he care if the bills are paid or not, so you are also looking at losing your house. You grew up under abuse, so there isn't any help from your family.

Out of desperation, you call a ministry to pray for you; you talk to your minister; and you share your problem(s) with other people. These people pray and share God's Words with you. Their prayers do help, and things begin to get better. Let's say, your husband comes home unexpectedly and he actually gives you some money to pay bills. You begin to believe that God's Words do help. This would be **Mark 4:5, 16** taking place in your life.

"And some feel on stony ground, where it had not much
earth; and immediately it sprang up, because it had no
depth of earth:"

Mark 4:5

"And these are they likewise which are sown on stony
ground; who, when they have heard the word, immediately
receive it with gladness;"

Mark 4:16

But you have NOT been taught how to study your answers, nor do
you even know it is a requirement to do so. Therefore, your answers
have NOT taken a deep root on the inside of your heart and body.
And without the root to fight off your circumstances, they will begin
to return again. Satan is NOT going to give up so easily.

Again, when Jesus was tempted in the wilderness, Luke tells us in
Luke 4:13 Satan only left Jesus alone for a season. Then he returned
again and fought with Jesus for the rest of His ministry. If you don't
believe the Holy Spirit, turn to **Matthew, Mark, Luke** and **John**;
read with an open mind how Satan used the scribes and Pharisees to
torture Jesus!

Our Master tells us, if Satan used people to torture and persecute
Him, then it doesn't matter who you are, he (Satan) is going to use
people to try us as well (**Matthew Ch. 10** & **John 15:18-20**).

He tells us in **John 16:1-5** that He is telling us these things ahead of
time so when they do happen to us, we will be expecting them and
not caught off balance, or offended.

Thus, the lady's situation will begin to return to her again. For example, let's say, all of a sudden, her husband was offended at work. So after going to the bar for a drink, he decided to go home and take his frustration out on his wife. And she was abused again.

This would be one of her trials which will try her faith. And without being firmly rooted in Jesus' Words, she will become discouraged and begin to doubt the ministries' help. This act causes the Christian to become offended towards Christians, and/or God, and the scriptures. This would be **Matthew 13:21; Mark 4:17 & Luke 8:13** taking place in the lady's life.

> "Yet hath he not root in himself, but dureth for a while: for when tribulation or persecution ariseth because of the word, by and by he is offended."

> **Matthew 13:21**

> "They on the rock are they, which, when they hear, receive the word with joy; and these have no root, which for a while believe, and in time of temptation fall away".

> **Luke 8:13**

You need to know, no one on the face of the earth can get you out of your problems completely, because these people are NOT you! They cannot DO the required studying for YOU. They cannot plant your answers from your mind down into your heart for you. You are required to do this work on your own because this is the only way YOU will be able to change YOUR mind, YOUR attitude, and YOUR offense towards God and Jesus' answers to your problems.

Jesus tells you in the verses of the sower, if there is NO ROOT on the inside of your heart, you will keep your help from the ministries and your Bible promises for only a little while. But when you are tested by (1) your persecutors or tribulations, (for an example, the abusive husband): (2) your affliction (for an example, your sickness): (3) your temptation to stop believing (for an example, waiting for the phone call to see if you received the employment or not): what will you do to combat the problem? You need the words of your promise to surface into your mind to win your victory.

This is how the lady with the issue of blood won her victory (**Luke 8:43-44**). She was forbidden to walk among the Jewish people by her law (**Leviticus 15:19**). This is why she was afraid to tell Jesus it was she who touched Him (**Luke 8:44-47**). But she was MORE concentrated on Jesus' Words of healing, than she was on being punished for breaking the Jewish law (**Luke 8:43-44**). And because she took this stand against her tribulation, she won her victory (**Luke 8:48**). This is the way we will win ours.

> "But he that received seed into the good ground is he that heareth the word, and understandeth it; which also beareth fruit, and bringeth forth, some an hundredfold, some sixty, some thirty."

Matthew 13:23

If you think this act can be accomplished without studying, you are just fooling yourself. Jesus' Words are true and they will work in your life. And if you try to complete **Matthew 13:23** without doing **Matthew 6:33**, when your same problem hits you square in the face all over again, *__you will buckle because there is NO root__*! This buckling will allow your state of affairs to return back on top of you once more.

YOU ARE the ONE who will have to choose whether or not you want to overcome **your** trials (**Joshua 24:15**)! There is no one else on the face of the earth who can make this choice for **you** (**Psalm 25:12**). Even God cannot make up **your** mind for **you** (**Proverbs 1:29; 3:31 & Isaiah 65:12**).

Trials are going to attack *YOU* personally (**Matthew 13:21; Mark 4:17 & Luke 8:13**). And if you refuse to seek God's Kingdom by meditating first (**Joshua 1:8 & Matthew 6:33**); then there will be no root on the inside of you. Again, without your root, there will be no strength on the inside of you to overcome your personal trials (**Matthew 13:21; Mark 4:17 & Luke 8:13**).

The Holy Spirit realizes He is repeating Himself THREE TIMES. This was done for a good reason. He wants you to know, this is NOT just a nice chapter to read. It needs to be taken seriously.

When we DO study by looking up all the scriptures which pertain to our Bible promise and we start to change our mind(s) and understand God and Jesus' perspective on life, doing this study causes us to become approved by God and Jesus (**II Timothy 2:14-15**). (1) It causes us to seek God's Kingdom in God and Jesus' way of life (**John 3:1-5 & 14:6**). (2) It causes us to comprehend God and Jesus' pathway to our VICTORY in life (**Psalm 81:10-16; Matthew 4:1-11; 13:15; & Luke 4:1-13**). (3) It causes us to change the way we think about life and transforms our thinking into God and Jesus' way (**Isaiah 55:7-11; Matthew 11:28-30; John 15:15; 16:25; Romans 12:2; I Corinthians 2:16; Ephesians 4:21-24 & Titus 3:5**). (4) It causes our mind(s) to get in tune with the Holy Spirit! Once this happens we can start to hear God's revelation knowledge. (5) Once we receive the revelation knowledge, it is ***only this kind of knowledge that the gates of hell cannot prevail against***. All other knowledge can be defeated by Satan, because the world's knowledge comes from him (**Genesis 3:5-6; & Matthew 16:13-19**). (6) After we receive our own personal revelation knowledge from God Himself, then NO demon in hell can rob our Bible answer(s) from our heart(s) and mind(s) (**Matthew 13:10-19**). (7) If we will follow God's instruction revealed to us, then we will gain our VICTORY over Satan's attacks in life (**Deuteronomy 28:1-14**).

However, there is one stipulation. We cannot give our victory away by helping the people who are not for God (**II Chronicles 18:1-19:2 & Matthew 7:6**). By doing so, it will cause us to fail in life. Turn to **Genesis Ch. 11:31-21:2** and read about Abraham's life. It wasn't until after his father died and Lot's family **was out** of Abraham's life that Sarah was allowed to have Isaac.

Jesus didn't get His victory over Satan until after He went to the cross and left His loved ones on this earth (**Matthew Ch. 28; Mark Ch.16; Luke Ch. 24 & John Ch. 20**). We are NOT stronger than Jesus (**Matthew 28:18**). And if He had to say good-by to His beloved mother in **John 19:26-27** to win His victory over Satan, then we must follow in His footsteps and do as He did (**Matthew 10:34-38 & Luke 14:26-27**).

(This is just a note, if your family is for God just as much as you are, then it is okay to stay together. Read **Luke 12:52-53**: the family members who agree with one another stay together. This is proven out in Abraham's case. Sarah and Abraham stay together because they agreed with one another).

After we study and do begin to get God's promise rooted down into our hearts, then it is time to be tested. Doing the law is God's way of testing us. So in our next lesson let's find out why we must do the law.

CHAPTER 7

Doing the Law

I N CHAPTER 2, THE Holy Spirit impressed me to give you some truths, which He would like to verify in the next four lessons. He (the Holy Spirit) had said, Paul told us in **Romans 2:13**, if we refuse to do God's law we will NOT be justified by Jesus. The church body just doesn't understand the fact that Jesus cannot justify us if we refuse to do God's law. This is because we will continue to sin if we don't complete the law in our lives (**Proverbs 1:22-33; Ezekiel 18:21-24 & John 8:34, 43-44**). Jesus refuses to justify the person who _**continues to sin.**_

Matthew 5:17-20, 21-26, 27-30, 38-45; 6:14-15, 24-33; 7:12-14, 15-20, 21-23, 24-27; 8:10-12; 10:34-38, 39-40; 12:25-37, 43-45; 13:18-22, 37-42, 48-50; 15:13-14, 16-20; 16:24-27; 18:3-20, 23-35; 19:17-22; 22:1-7, 8-13; 24:43-51; 25:1-13, 14-30 & 31-46 are all Jesus' WORDS. There are 30 different lessons recorded. Every one of these lessons tells the Christian they will **not** be justified by Jesus if he/she continues to sin from their flesh! Some of Jesus' Words are clear and some are not. Let the Holy Spirit grant you His revealed knowledge on our Lord's lessons.

The scriptures recorded are only Matthew's account of Jesus' truth. Mark, Luke and John also show this same fact (verified by Jesus' Words) in their books as well. We are going to examine the fact that Jesus refuses to justify the person who continues to sin; from **Matthew's** account in **8:12; 13:40-41**, from **Luke's** account in **12:45-46**, from **John's** account in **8:34-35** and from **I John 1:7**.

Y'shua *has* the right to refuse to justify us!! We are the ONES who need to be justified, because *WE are the sinners*!! Jesus went through the SAME temptations to sin as we are living through in today's world (**Hebrews 2:18 & 4:15**).

> "For we have not an high priest which cannot be touched with the feeling of our infirmities: *but was in all points tempted like as we are*, . . ."

Hebrews 4:15

> "For in that he *himself hath suffered being tempted*, . . ."

Hebrews 2:18A

> "Ye are they which have *continued with me in my temptations*."

Luke 22:28

> "And when the devil had ended all the temptation, he departed from him *for a season*."

Luke 4:13

Our Master was tempted to SIN in the same way we are tempted to SIN. And yet, He never once gave into His temptations.

"For we have not an high priest which cannot be touched with the feeling of our infirmities: but was in all points tempted like as we are, *yet without sin.*"

Hebrews 4:15

"*Which of you convinceth me of sin*? And if I say the truth, why do ye not believe me?"

John 8:46

Our LORD *IS the precious Lamb of God who is worthy to be honored* because He went through the SAME temptations to sin as we do today: And He wanted to sin as much as you and I want to sin (**Matthew 4:1-12; Luke 4:1-13; 22:28; Hebrews 5:7 & 12:1-4**). But, He *didn't sin*. He suffered in hell as though He **did** sin, because He was suffering our payment for our sins (**Acts 2:25-28, 31; 13:35; Psalm 16:10; Galatians 3:13 & I Peter 3:18-20**).

But because He **didn't sin**, He was able to defeat Satan in Satan's own territory (**Psalm 16:10 & Acts 2:25-27, 31; 13:35**). He took the keys of hell and of death while He was down there (**Revelation 1:18**). Then, He rose again, to give us **our** life (**Revelation Ch. 5**).

So, if He is the ONE who decides to refuse to justify us because we are still sinning before His face, then He has the RIGHT to do so!! And there is nothing on the face of the earth we can do to change Jesus' decision!!

We MUST stop sinning from our flesh, before Jesus will use His blood to cleanse us from our sin.

"***But if we walk in the light, as he is in the light***, we have fellowship one with another, and ***the blood of Jesus Christ his Son cleanseth us from all sin.***"

I John 1:7

John tells us in **I John 1:7** we MUST walk in the light, the very SAME way Jesus is in the light, ***before*** Jesus can and will cleanse us from our sin.

So how is Jesus in the light?

"So Christ was once offered to bear the sins of many; and unto them that look for him shall he appear ***the second time without sin*** unto salvation."

Hebrews 9:28

He is in the light WITHOUT the SIN. We are told that we must walk in the light in the SAME way Jesus is in the light. He had to bear our sins the first time He came to this earth, but He overcame the sins He was bearing. So, He is NOW in the light WITHOUT our SINS. And again, we are told to be in the light in the SAME way in which Jesus is in the light now. Therefore, we MUST walk in the light without the sin BEFORE Jesus will cleanse us from our sins (**I John 1:7**).

Don't you remember? God and Jesus CHOSE ***not to go against our will(s)*** (**Genesis Ch. 3; Joshua 24:15; Ruth 1:15-16; I Kings 18:21; II Kings 17:39-41; John 8:34** & **Romans 6:16**)! This is one of the main reasons why Jesus cannot justify us unless ***we choose*** to stop sinning.

Each time you CHOOSE to sin, you are showing your LORD God and your Master Jesus Christ your sin is MORE important to you than They are to you (**Genesis Ch. 3; II Kings 17:39-41; John 8:34 & Romans 6:16**). Therefore, you are showing Them that you are MORE WILLING to sin, than you are WILLING to do God's law (**Romans 6:16D**). Hence, because you are still sinning, it becomes your WILL to sin when you _**DO**_ sin (**Genesis 3:6; Numbers 13:25-14:4; John 8:34 & Romans 6:16D**). Consequently, Jesus will NOT violate your WILL by cleansing you from the sin you are so _willing_ to do (**I John 1:7**)!

Y'shua is leaving the choice up to YOU as to whether you CHOOSE to DO His Words or not (**Matthew 5:19; 7:24-27; Luke 6:46; & John 14:23-24**)! If you choose to do Jesus' Words, you are doing God's law (**Deuteronomy 18:18-19; John 12:49-50 & Romans 6:16E**). And the act of doing God's law in your life will cause you to stop sinning (**Deuteronomy 28:1-14; Ezekiel 18:21 & Matthew 19:21**). But, if you do _**not**_ choose to do Jesus' Words (the law); you will continue to serve your sin (**Matthew 19:22 & John 8:34**). And, in God and Jesus' eyes you will remain the _same_ as the sinner (**Matthew 12:30 & John 8:34**)!!

> "Know ye not, that _**to whom ye yield yourselves servants to obey**_, his servants ye are to whom ye obey; _**whether of sin unto death,**_ or of obedience unto righteousness?"

> **Romans 6:16**

You can yield yourselves to become Jesus' servant by DOING His Words (**John 12:26**). Doing Jesus' Words (God's law) will cause you to STOP sinning (**Romans 6:16D**). Or you can yield yourselves to become the servant of your own sin, by continuing to sin (**Romans 6:16C**). But if you do, there is a price to pay. Read Jesus' words in **John 8:34 & Matthew 13:40-41**.

"Jesus answered them, *Verily, verily, I say unto you, Whosoever, committeth sin is the servant of sin.*"

John 8:34

Meditate on our Lord's words in **John 8:34**. He is telling us, as long as we are choosing to give into our sin by sinning, we will always obey what our sin wants us to do. This fact causes us to become the servants to our own sin (**John 8:34**)

"Know ye not, that *to whom ye yield yourselves servants to obey, his servants ye are* to whom ye obey; whether of *sin unto death*, . . .".

Romans 6:16A-C

As a result, because we are still sinning and servants to our sin, we remain the SAME as the sinner in God and Jesus' eyes (**Matthew 12:30** & **Luke 6:45-46**). Sin is very offensive to God, Jesus and the Holy Spirit (**Ezekiel 18:20; Matthew 13:40-43** & **25:31-46**). Therefore it is JESUS who will send forth HIS angels at the END of the world (**Matthew 13:40-41A**). It is JESUS who will have HIS angels REMOVE from HIS KINGDOM, ALL Christians which are offending the Holy Spirit and HIM (**Matthew 13:41B**). And it is JESUS who will have the Christians who are still doing the iniquity REMOVED from HIS KINGDOM as well (**Matthew 13:41C**). Remember people!! Outright sinners are NOT allowed to be on the inside of God and Jesus' Kingdom (**John 3:36**). It is ONLY the Christian who has truly been born again who is allowed to be on the inside and a part of God and Jesus' Kingdom (**John 3:3-5**).

Think about it. YOU must belong and be on the inside of a club, building, room, or kingdom BEFORE you can be removed from it. The person who isn't truly BORN AGAIN, IS NOT on the inside of God and Jesus' Kingdom: and does NOT belong to Their Kingdom (**John Ch. 3**). Thus, you CANNOT be removed from a Kingdom that you do NOT belong to or you are NOT in. In other words, YOU MUST BE BORN AGAIN and on the inside of God and Jesus' Kingdom, BEFORE you can be removed and taken out of that Kingdom!!

> "As therefore the tares are gathered and burned in the fire; *so shall it be in the end of this world*. The Son of man shall send forth his angels, and ***they shall gather out of his kingdom*** all things that offend, ***and them which do iniquity;***"

Matthew 13:40-41

Again, meditate on Jesus' words in **Matthew 13:40-41.** Catch the revelation! Jesus did ***not*** say that His angels would gather the people who claim they are born again and are not, out of His Kingdom. He said, He would have His angels gather ALL things which offend Him, and the people who do iniquity, out of His Kingdom. It doesn't matter if you are Christian or not, if you are still doing the iniquity when He returns, you will be removed from His Kingdom.

As long as you choose to do the iniquity (sin) in front of the Holy Spirit and Jesus' face, you are offending Them. And according to His Words in **Matthew 13:40-42**, He will not forgive you, nor change you in the twinkle of an eye, at the end of the world. He ***will not*** take you to heaven (**Matthew 13:40-42; 25:1-12, 31-46** & **Luke 12:42-46**)!

But, He will judge and reward you as according to the type of work you have completed while you have lived on this earth.

> "For the Son of man shall come in the glory of his Father with his angels; and then he shall reward every man according to his works."

> **Matthew 16:27**

> "But and if that servant say in his heart, My lord delayeth his coming: and shall begin to beat the menservants and maidens, and to eat and drink, and to be drunken; The lord of that servant will come in a day when he looketh not for him, and at an hour when he is not aware, and will cut him in sunder, ***and will appoint him his portion with the unbelievers.***"

> **Luke 12:45-46**

You must be a believer to be able to be thrown in with the unbelievers. There are only two kinds of people when it comes to God. You are either a believer, or an unbeliever (**John Ch. 3**). There is no person who claims to be a believer, but is not for real. The wolf in sheep's clothing believes in God and Jesus and is in the Kingdom of God. But, they believe and teach wrong doctrine (**Matthew 7:15-20; John 10:5, 12-13** & **II Timothy 4:1-4**). And it is these true born again believers who believe doctrine which is different from Jesus' Words, and do the words they believe, who will be removed from God and Jesus' Kingdom. This is because this wrong doctrine allows the believers to remain sinners in God and Jesus' eyes (**II Timothy 4:1-4** & **Revelation Ch. 2-3**).

"But he answered and said, Every plant which my heavenly Father halt not planted, shall be rooted up. Let them alone: they be blind leaders of the blind. And if the blind lead the blind, both shall fall into the ditch."

Matthew 15:13-14

Think about Jesus' Words and your denomination's words. Does your church's doctrine believe and do what Jesus tells His church to do? Do the words agree all the time? If they do not agree all the time, then Jesus tells us that we are against Him.

"He that is not with me is against me; and he that gathereth not with me scattereth abroad."

Matthew 12:30

In other words Jesus considers these people to be unfaithful to Him because they do NOT agree with Him and His Words all the time (**Matthew 12:30; 15:13-14; John 12:48; Acts 3:23 & Revelation Ch. 2-3**). Therefore, when Jesus tells us in **Luke 12:46** that He will cast the believers in with the unbelievers because they have not been faithful to Him, this truth causes **Matthew 13:40-43** to agree with **Luke 12:46**. **Matthew 13:40-42; 16:27; 25:31-32 & Luke 12:46** all agree when they tell us Jesus will judge His believers when He does return to this earth. In other words, when Jesus does return to this earth, the *first thing He will do*, is to judge His church on how they have lived their lives on this earth (**Matthew 16:27**).

"When the Son of man shall come in his glory, and all the holy angels with him, then shall he sit upon the throne of his glory: And before him shall be gathered all nations: and

he shall separate them one from another, as a shepherd
divideth his sheep from the goats:"

Matthew 25:31-32

If Jesus judges His people to be unfaithful to Him, then His angels will
cast His believers with the unbelievers. According to **I Corinthians
12:3**, people CANNOT call Jesus LORD unless they do have the
Holy Spirit living on the inside of their bodies!! You are NOT allowed
to have the Holy Spirit living on the inside of your body unless you
are a true believer (**John Ch. 3** & **I Corinthians 2:10-16**).

In **Matthew 7:21-23** & **25:1-12** there are true believers who *were
not faithful* to Jesus. We can know these people are true believers,
because they do have the permission to call Jesus their LORD. In
other words, these people cannot claim that they believe and really
they don't believe in Jesus. They could not call Jesus LORD if they
didn't really believe that Jesus was God's Son and that He died for
them (**John 3:16**). It is these true believers who Jesus tells to depart
from Him because He doesn't know them. When He leaves these
believers on the outside of His Kingdom, there is no other place
where they can live, except to be left with the unbelievers in this
earth (**Luke 12:43-46**).

According to Jesus' Words in **Matthew 13:40-42**: these people were
NOT faithful to Jesus because they were and are still doing the
iniquity when Jesus returns to this earth.

"The Son of man shall send forth his angels, and they shall
gather out of his kingdom all things that offend, *and them
which do iniquity*:"

Matthew 13:41

"And then will I profess unto them, I never knew you:
depart from me, *ye that work iniquity*."

Matthew 7:23

Until **Matthew 25:1-12** is explained in a future chapter it is not as
clear as Jesus' Words in **Matthew 13:41** & **7:23**; but Jesus is also
telling these believers to depart from Him because they did not do
the work which will cause them to stop sinning (to stop doing the
iniquity) (**Matthew 25:7-12**). In other words, Jesus doesn't consider
you to be faithful to Him, unless you do the work which causes you
to stop sinning! As long as you are doing the iniquity, (sinning), you
are considered by Jesus to be a servant to your sin.

"Jesus answered them, Verily, verily, I say unto you,
Whosoever committeth sin is the servant of sin."

John 8:34

As long as you chose to serve your sin by giving into it and do the
iniquity, you will remain your sin's servant.

"Know ye not, *that to whom ye yield yourselves servants to
obey*, his servants ye are to whom ye obey; *whether of sin
unto death*, . . ."

Romans 6:16A-C

As long as you remain your sin's servant, you will NOT live in God's
house forever.

"*And the servant abideth NOT in the house for ever*, but the Son abideth ever."

John 8:35

As **Romans 6:16A-C** tells us, as long as we are serving our own sin, we will end our lives in death.

> "But when the righteous turneth away from his righteousness and committeth iniquity, and doeth according to all the abominations that the wicked man doeth, shall he live? All his righteousness that he hath done shall not be mentioned: in his trespass that he hath trespassed, and in his sin that he hath sinned, in them shall he die."

Ezekiel 18:24

This scripture does apply to the born again believer of today's world, if he/she does NOT stop sinning. We are told in **Matthew 7:23; 13:41-42; 25:1-12; Luke 12:45-46; John 8:34-35; & Romans 6:16A-C** as long as we do the iniquity in our lives we will NOT be allowed to stay in God and Jesus' Kingdom. We will be cast out of Their Kingdom when Jesus returns to this earth to judge us (**Matthew 7:21-23; 13:40-42; 16:27; 25:31-46; Luke 12:46 & John 8:35**). What do you think will happen to the believers who are left to suffer with the unbelievers? The only chance they have is to face the Antichrist and stay faithful to Jesus.

> "And it was given unto him to make war with the saints and to overcome them: and power was given him over all kindreds, and tongues, and nations."

Revelation 13:7

The saints are the believers. Yes, there will be people who will accept Jesus during this period of time. But the saints also mean the people who have been left to live with the unbelievers and to deal with the Antichrist.

> "Every tree that bringeth not forth good fruit is hewn down, and cast into the fire."

Matthew 7:19

> "If a man abide NOT in me, he is cast forth as a branch, and is withered; and men gather them, and cast them into the fire, and they are burned."

John 15:6

This fire is the furnace of fire which forces the saint to face the Antichrist.

> "The Son of man shall send forth his angels, and they shall gather out of his kingdom all things that offend, and them which do iniquity; And *shall cast them into a furnace of fire*: there shall be wailing and gnashing of teeth."

Matthew 13:41-42

> "The lord of that servant will come in a day when he looketh not for him, and at an hour when he is not aware, and will cut him in sunder, and *will appoint him his portion with the unbelievers*."

Luke 12:46

"And to you who are troubled rest with us, when the Lord Jesus shall be revealed from heaven with his mighty angels, In flaming fire taking vengeance on them that know not God, ***and that obey not the gospel of our Lord Jesus Christ***: Who shall be punished with everlasting destruction from the presence of the Lord, and from the glory of his power;"

II Thessalonians 1:7-9

Just because you have accepted Jesus as your savoir and this fact causes you to belong to the kingdom of God; this is NOT a guarantee you will be allowed to stay in God and Jesus' Kingdom.

"***But the children of the kingdom shall be cast out into outer darkness***: there shall be weeping and gnashing of teeth."

Matthew 8:12

Does this sound as if Jesus is going to justify us just because we have accepted Him as our savior (**Romans 2:13 & 3:31**)? It would be so much easier to serve Jesus by doing His Words now (**John 15:1-5**). This act would cause you to do God's law (**Matthew 5:17-20**), God's Will (**Matthew 7:21**), Jesus' gospel (**Matthew 4:23**), and the "fruit of the Spirit" (**Galatians 5:14-23**) all at the same time. Plus, doing Jesus' Words will cause you to stop sinning.

"Know ye not, ***that to whom ye yield yourselves servants to obey, his servants ye are*** to whom ye obey; whether of sin unto death, ***or of obedience unto righteousness***?"

Romans 6:16

This is why we are commanded by Jesus to do His Words (God's law) in **Matthew 5:17-20; 7:21-23** & **John 13:34; 15:1-5, 12-13**!! It is NOT impossible to do!!

"For with God nothing shall be impossible."

Luke 1:37

In our next chapter, let's begin to study how we are to do Jesus' Words.

Un-Answered Prayers

T HE HOLY SPIRIT SHOWED us in our last chapter, if we refuse to do God's law we **_cannot_** be justified by Jesus. We MUST be able to be justified by Jesus, in front of God first, before He can: (1) allow us into heaven (**Matthew 7:21** & **Revelation 21:27**); (2) allow us to prosper (**Proverbs 13:22** & **28:13**); and (3) be set free to answer our prayers (**Isaiah 57:17; 59:1-3** & **John 9:31**). Read **John 9:31** carefully. God will not hear the prayer of sinners. The sinner must complete two requirements before God will hear their prayers. You must be a worshipper of God and _you MUST do God's Will._

> "Now we know that God heareth not sinners: but if any man be a worshipper of God, **_and doeth his will, him he heareth_**."

> **John 9:31**

There is too much scripture to study to prove how we are to worship God. But we will study how we are required to do God's Will in a future chapter. Nevertheless, because many of today's church people have not been taught that God cannot answer our prayers if we are **_not_** justified by Jesus first, the Holy Spirit will start with this fact.

Remember, if we are not justified, then this causes us to be considered by God to be the SAME as the sinner. Thus, we are told in **Isaiah 57:17; 59:1-3** and **John 9:31**, because our sins are in God's way, He has turned His face away from us and cannot answer our prayers.

Ezekiel 18:20 and **Romans 6:23** tell us God cannot honor sin. Therefore, as long as we continue to sin, He cannot answer our prayers totally, because He would be honoring the sin which lives on the inside of us (**John 8:34; Romans 5:12 & James 4:1-3**). This is why He turns His face away from us when we are praying to Him (**Isaiah 57:17**). This fact is true because we would use God's answers to help our sins (**James 4:1-3**). This would force God to honor our sin instead of helping US.

> "Ye lust, and have not: ye kill, and desire to have, and cannot obtain: ye fight and war, yet ye have not, because ye ask not. *Ye ask, and receive not, because ye ask amiss,* **that ye may consume it upon your lusts**."

> **James 4:2-3**

We MUST stop sinning before God can answer our prayers in the way we want Him to answer us (**James 4:1-3 & John 15:16**). The Holy Spirit didn't say our prayers would NOT be answered. He just said they would NOT be answered in the WAY we are looking for them to be answered!!

There are a lot of people who are having trouble understanding how we would use "God's answers" to our prayers to help our sins (**James 4:1-3**). Let the Holy Spirit explain. Since we are studying how to receive "God's Prosperity", let's use money as an illustration.

Let's say you are asking God to make you very rich financially. But, you haven't repented on the way you use your money. You buy things which are way too expensive for your budget; you eat out and/or travel on credit; or you buy little things you can't afford. In other words, you go into debt easily. And, let's say, God does answer your prayers and He does make you very rich while you are doing these things.

Since you are now wealthy, how are you going to handle your funds? You may tell yourself, you will tithe and you will control your funds in a responsible manner. But, if you cannot control your sinning habits before God answers your prayer; then you will never be able to control them after He answers you (**John 8:34** & **James 4:1-3**).

John 8:34 tells us as long as we continue to give into our fleshly wants by sinning, then we will always be a servant to our sins. This means we will always do what our sin wants us to do whether God answers our prayers or not (**James 4:3**).

Consequently, because your sin is still in control of your finances, when you become prosperous you will end up using your money in wrong ways and lose all you gained (**John 8: 34; Romans 6:16** & **James 4:3**). This would be you using God's answer to your prayer on your lusts (sin) (**James 4:3**). Therefore, you would be forcing God to honor your sin instead of helping you. And He will NOT honor *SIN* (**Ezekiel 18:20; Isaiah 42:8;** & **Romans 6:23**)!! Thus, He will NOT cause you to prosper, while you are still sinning (**James 4:2-3** & **Deuteronomy 8:18**).

So you do not think the Holy Spirit is picking on the poor people who are praying for "God's Prosperity", let's use another example.

Let's say God chose to answer the prayer of a single person who asked to receive a mate. One of the reasons a person who is single cannot find a mate is because marriage requires the person to change. If you really want your marriage to work, the person must change from being selfish to being determined to give the "fruits of the Spirit" all the time. In other words, right now he/she is MORE interested in making life better and easier for himself, or herself, than he/she is in being kind to other people (**Matthew 16:24-26**).

If God would answer his/her prayer and give them a mate before the person learned how to give the "fruits of the Spirit", he/she would remain selfish in the marriage. This situation would cause big arguments. The couple would end up either fighting all the time or they would get divorced. (Remember, it is the "*hardness of heart*" God hates in the divorce, NOT the divorce itself) (**Matthew 19:3-8**). In other words, it is the person who refuses to cooperate with Jesus' Words who has the hard heart (**John 12:48**). And it is this hardness of heart God hates, not the people, or the fact a divorce was necessary.

(This is just a note. There are single people who want to marry and they do perform the "fruits of the Spirit" in their lives. Many times these people are serving in ministry. There are people who Jesus reserves as eunuchs for the kingdom of heaven, even though they want to marry. These people don't know it, but they agreed to this kind of life for Jesus' sake and they will be rewarded GREATLY because they have suffered in this way!! Be comforted, you are serving Jesus (**Matthew 19:8-9**)!!

Let's return to the examples of the people who have not stopped sinning. These two situations would be examples of using God's answer to our prayers on the Christian's own lusts (**James 4:1-3**). In other words, in the examples, these people would be using their sin of being selfish and irresponsible on God's answer to their prayers

(**James 4:3**). Therefore, God would have answered *their sin* instead of answering THEM.

The Holy Spirit is not picking on you! He is just showing you how you would use God's answer to your prayers on your own lusts, if you refuse to change. **James 4:1-3** applies to everyone and every situation which involves unanswered and answered prayers. While the Christian continues to sin, their main prayer cannot be answered (**James 4:3**). It is *not* just with these two examples.

Therefore, if you WANT your prayers answered in the way you are looking for them to be answered, DO the "fruits of the Spirit". (The "fruits of the Spirit" is the law and God's Will completed in the Christian's life)! When you decide to do the "fruits of the Spirit" you will STOP sinning! Then God can be set free to answer your prayers (**John 15:16**). Let's study this fact from the scriptures.

Jesus tells us in **John 15:16** we MUST produce the "fruits of the Spirit", and we MUST cause them to remain, *before* we can ask whatsoever we will.

> "Ye have not chosen me, but I have chosen you, and ordained you, *that ye should go and bring forth fruit, and that your fruit should remain*: . . ."

> **John 15:16A-E**

Jesus tells us in this verse He has chosen us from among the world's people. And, He tells us He has ordained us to bring forth fruit. What kind of fruit is Jesus telling us we MUST produce?

Remember, Jesus is telling us to bring forth the fruit from the inside of our bodies. We can know this is true because of Jesus' Words in **Matthew 7:15-20; 12:33-37; Luke 6:42-45; John 15:1-6, 16** and James' words in **James Ch.3**. Any time Jesus talks about fruit, He talks about the kind of fruit we produce with our *words*.

So again let's return to **John 15:16**. We are told to bring forth fruit and to cause our fruit to remain before we can ask the desires of our heart and our prayer will be answered.

> "Ye have not chosen me, but I have chosen you, and ordained you, that ye should go and bring forth fruit, and that your fruit should remain: . . ."

John 15:16A-E

Why should it remain?

> ". . . that whatsoever ye shall ask of the Father in my name, he may give it you."

John 15:16F

We know from Jesus' Words in **Matthew 7:15-20; 12:33-37; Luke 6:42-45** and James' words from **James Ch.3**, it is the fruit which comes from our words that Jesus wants us to produce.

So, since we know that it is the fruit from our words that Jesus is looking for, what kind of fruit does He want?

> "Every tree that bringeth **not** forth **GOOD** fruit is hewn down, and cast into the fire."

Matthew 7:19

Jesus is looking for us to produce the **"GOOD"** fruit from our words.

We can know what kind of GOOD FRUIT Jesus is talking about in **John 15:16** and in **Matthew 7:19** because of His words in **Matthew 12:33**. He tells us we are to make *our tree* GOOD, and *our fruit* GOOD, or else our tree and its fruit WILL be corrupt.

> "Either make the tree good, and his fruit good; or else make the tree corrupt, and his fruit corrupt: for the tree is known by his fruit."

Matthew 12:33

Our tree which produces our fruit lives on the inside of our bodies. We can know this is true because of Jesus' next three sentences in **Matthew 12:34-36**. He tells us it is the words which come out of *our mouth(s)* that show us whether our fruit is GOOD or bad.

> "O Generation of vipers, how can ye, being evil, speak good things? For out of the abundance of the heart the mouth speaketh. A good man out of the good treasure of the heart bringeth forth good things, and an evil man out of the evil treasure bringeth forth evil things. But I say unto you, That every idle word that men shall speak, they shall give account thereof in the day of judgment."

Matthew 12:34-36

Our Master is looking for us to produce the "Good" fruit from our words.

There are many people who have been taught that Jesus is looking for us to produce the fruit of getting people saved, when He talks about bringing forth the fruit. And yes this is good. But, people cannot be the "Good" fruit Jesus is referring to in **Matthew 7:19** and in **John 15:16**. Because, in **Matthew 19:17**; in **Mark 10:18** and in **Luke 18:19** our Lord tells us, the ONLY "ONE" who is good is GOD, Himself!! Therefore, the people who live on this earth are NOT considered by God as being the "GOOD" fruit Jesus is referring to in **Matthew 7:19** and in **John 15:16**.

Besides, YOU cannot force the fruit of the saved people to remain "GOOD". If they want to change their minds about God, there is nothing you can do. The only kind of fruit which YOU can cause to remain "GOOD" is the fruit which comes from YOU. You only have control over your OWN words and actions!!

So, what kind of "GOOD" fruit and words is it, which Jesus is looking for us to produce in **Matthew 7:19** & **John 15:16**?

Ephesians 5:9 gives us the answer.

> **"(For the fruit of the Spirit is in all goodness and righteousness and truth;)"**

> **Ephesians 5:9**

And, again, we are told in **Ephesians 5:9**, the "fruits of the Spirit" is the ***only kind of fruit*** which is GOOD. Consequently, Jesus has to be discussing the "good fruits of the Spirit" in **Matthew 7:19** and in **John 15:16**. He tells us we MUST produce it in our lives or we will be cast into the fire. He also tells us in **John 15:2, 6**, if we end our lives in this fire, *we will burn*!

We went through all this truth just to let you know what kind of fruit Jesus is telling us we must produce in **John 15:16**. It has to be the "fruit of the Spirit" because this is the only kind of fruit which brings forth the credit of being judged *good* by God. Now let's read our scripture again.

> "Ye have not chosen me, but I have chosen you, and ordained you, that *ye should go and bring forth fruit, and that your fruit should remain*: . . ."

John 15:16A-E

From our study in **Matthew 7:19** & **12:32-36** we found out what kind of fruit we must produce, but what does Jesus mean when He tells us it has to remain?

Let's take a look at the fruits.

> "But the fruit of the Spirit is love, joy, peace, longsuffering, gentleness, goodness, faith, Meekness, temperance: against such there is no law."

Galatians 5:22-23

So YOU have decided on the inside of yourself, you are going to produce the fruits from the inside out. Hence, you resolved to give the gentleness and goodness today. As a result, God will start giving you opportunities to produce this fruit by giving you situations to live through. This circumstance is just one example of two of the fruits.

Let's say, a friend asked you to get him/her a cup of coffee, but it didn't suit you at the time you were asked. You now have a choice to make! Are you going to give love and go out of your way to serve your friend the coffee (**Galatians 5:22** & **Matthew 5:44** & **7:12**)? Or, are you going to complain about how the favor will inconvenience you?

The choice to get the coffee without allowing yourself to complain, is giving the fruits of love, gentleness and goodness to your friend. This step will give you all kinds of good credit written by your name in heaven (**Revelation 20:12**).

But, if you choose to complain to yourself while you are getting the coffee; then doing the favor doesn't do you much good. Yes, you have the credit written by your name because you did the deed of serving your friend. This is producing the fruit of goodness which Jesus is requiring us to produce in **Matthew 5:44C** & in **John 15:16B**. This favor has been recorded by your name (**Revelation 20:12**). But the sin of complaining while you were performing the favor canceled out the credit of the "fruit of the Spirit" (**Ezekiel 18:24** & **Matthew 12:33-37**).

The "fruit of the Spirit" came with the service performed (**Ezekiel 18:21-23; Matthew 12:33-35** & **John 15:16A-E**). However, your complaining is sin (**Jude 15-16**). Sin cancels out the credit of the good fruit (**Ezekiel 18:24; Matthew 7:19; 12:33-37** & **John 15:16D**). Thus the credit of your fruit did _NOT remain_ by your name in (**John 15:16E**)!!

Jesus requires us to do the good "fruit of the Spirit" and to cause it to remain by our names _**before**_ God will answer our prayers.

> "Ye have not chosen me, but I have chosen you, and ordained you, _**that ye should go and bring forth fruit, and that your fruit should remain**_: . . ."

> **John 15:16A-E**

Why should this happen in our lives?

"*. . . that whatsoever ye shall ask of the Father in my name, he may give it you.*"

John 15:16F

Thus, Jesus requires us to STOP sinning by producing the "fruits of the Spirit"; *before,* God can answer our prayers in the way we want Him to answer them.

Since we MUST stop sinning if we want our prayers answered in the way it will help us; let's study one of Jesus' ways to stop sinning in the next chapter.

CHAPTER 9

Conquering Sin

I N OUR LAST CHAPTER, the Holy Spirit showed us the fact that we MUST stop sinning if we want God to be able to answer our prayers. In this lesson the Holy Spirit is going to show us one of God and Jesus' ways to help us stop.

Let's take the example given in the Holy Spirit's last lesson. Remember? Your friend asked you if you could get him/her a cup of coffee, <u>but the timetable didn't suit you</u>. Thus, you did the favor of getting the coffee, but complained because it was inconvenient for you to do so.

The Holy Spirit had said; if you are going to complain while you are getting your friend's coffee, then the credit of the "Fruit of the Spirit" is removed from your name. You may as well have told your friend it just didn't suit you to do the service at the time (**John 15:16A-D**).

You could tell your friend that it didn't suit you. Or you could get the coffee and complain. But, if you respond in either of these ways you will remain in your sin! The whole idea of inconveniencing you was to cause you to deny your sin, and tell it "**_No_**!"

God and Jesus wanted you to ***deny yourself*** the pleasure of complaining. They wanted you to ***deny yourself*** the pleasure of resenting the fact that you had to go out of your way to do the favor. They wanted you to *deny yourself* the pleasure of allowing yourself to become bitter. And, they wanted you to *deny yourself* the pleasure of wanting revenge for asking you at an inconvenient time. This is what Jesus means when He tells us to *deny ourselves*, pick up our cross and do as He did for us.

> "Then said Jesus unto his disciples, *If any man will come after me, let him deny himself, and take up his cross, and follow me.*"

> **Matthew 16:24**

Our LORD had to deny himself the pleasure of giving into these "flesh feelings" all the time (**Luke 22:28; Hebrews 2:18 & 4:15**). If He didn't have the same feelings that we have, then He could NOT have been tempted to do wrong just the same as we are tempted to do wrong (**James 1:13-14; Matthew 4:1-11; Luke 4:1-13; 22:28 & Hebrews 2:18**). Remember, James tells us we must be tempted by our own lust before we can be tempted to sin! Read James' words.

> "But every man is tempted, *when he is drawn away of his own lust,* and enticed."

> **James 1:14**

In other words, Jesus could have NOT been tempted to sin unless He was drawn away by *HIS OWN LUST* (**Matthew 4:1-11 & Luke 4:1-13**)!! BUT, Jesus *told HIS lust* "NO"!!! *NOW, He looks at YOU and He tells YOU to DO as He did for YOU*!!!

> "And when he had called the people unto him with his disciples also, he said unto them, *WHOSOEVER will come*

after me, let him deny himself, and take up his cross, and follow me."

Mark 8:34

"This is my commandment, That ye love one another, as I have loved you. Greater love hath no man than this, *that a man lay down his life for his friends."*

John 15:12-13

Jesus said "NO" to His sin life and laid it down for your sake (**James 1:14; Mark 8:34** & **John 15:13**). NOW, He is looking at YOU and telling YOU; "DO the SAME for ME and your friends, as I DID FOR YOU!!!"

"This is MY COMMANDMENT, That ye love one another, as I have loved you."

John 15:12

In other words, love your friend who asked you for the coffee in the VERY SAME WAY, as JESUS LOVED, AND LOVES YOU (**John 15:12**). He said "NO" to HIS flesh feelings for your sake, now it is your turn to SAY "NO" to your flesh feelings for Him and your friends' sake!!

"My sheep HEAR MY VOICE, and I know them, AND THEY FOLLOW ME:"

John 10:27

In other words, listen to and DO Jesus' Words instead of paying attention to other people, ministers, or anyone who speaks different words than what is written in the "Red".

> "And when he putteth forth his own sheep, he goeth before them, and the sheep follow him: for they know his voice. And a stranger will they not follow, but will flee from him: for they know not the voice of strangers."

John 10:4-5

And He tells us to DO AS HE DID for us.

> "This is my commandment, That ye love one another, as I have loved you. Greater love hath no man than this, that a man lay down his life for his friends."

John 15:12-13

You could say, "Greater love hath no man than this, that a man lay down his (sin life) for his friends."

This is what Jesus is asking YOU and me to DO.

> "And when he had called the people unto him with his disciples also, he said unto them, Whosoever will come after me, let him deny himself, and take up his cross, and follow me."

Mark 8:34

You could say Jesus said, whosoever will come after Jesus, (1) let him deny himself by denying his sin life for Jesus, as Jesus denied

His sin life for YOU (**Matthew 16:24-27; Mark 8:34;** & **John 15:13**).
(2) take up his cross of saying "NO" to his flesh and not allowing it to
have its own way, as Jesus didn't allow His flesh to have its own way
in His life (**Hebrews 12:1-4**). And, (3) treat your family and friends *in
Christ* in the very SAME WAY as Jesus treated His family and friends
who followed after Him (**Matthew 12:47-50; John 13:34** & **15:12**).
This is what **Matthew 16:24-27; Mark 8:34; John 13:34** & **15:12-13**
means!!! If you don't believe the Holy Spirit's interpretation of these
verses, try doing life YOUR WAY and see how far you get!!!

"There is a way which SEEMTH RIGHT unto a man, but
the end there of are the ways of death."

Proverbs 14:12

"The way of a FOOL is RIGHT IN HIS OWN EYES:
but he that hearkeneth unto counsel is wise."

Proverbs 12:15

This is HARD on your FLESH; the Holy Spirit knows this fact.
This is why Jesus told you in **Matthew 6:33;** in **Matthew 13:18,
20;** in **Mark 4:14, 16** and in **Luke 8:11, 13** to find a Bible promise
which MEANS MORE to YOU than anything else on this earth.
Study and meditate on your promise to the point in which it becomes
ROOTED down on the inside of your heart and mind. And then
determine on the inside of YOU that nothing on the face of this
earth is MORE important to you than your God-given promise!!
And when you are tempted to sin, then your Bible promise will come
to your memory and the sin just will NOT be as important to you
anymore. This is HOW Jesus overcame His desire to sin as well.
YOU BECAME MORE IMPORTANT TO HIM, than His sin

feelings were to Him. He resisted His own sin feelings to the POINT that He caused BLOOD to flow from His veins.

> "And being in an agony he prayed more earnestly: and his sweat was as it were great drops of blood falling down to the ground."

> **Luke 22:44**

> "Wherefore seeing we also are compassed about with so great a cloud of witnesses, let us lay aside every weight, *and the sin which doth so easily beset us*, and let us run with patience the race that is set before us, Looking unto Jesus the author and finisher of our faith; *who for the joy that was set before him* endured the cross, despising the shame, and is set down at the right hand of the throne of God. For consider him that endured such contradiction of sinners against himself, lest ye be wearied and faint in your minds. Ye have NOT YET RESISTED UNTO BLOOD, striving against sin."

> **Hebrews 12:1-4**

Therefore, when your friend asked you for a cup of coffee and the timetable didn't suit, **Hebrews 12:1-4** tells you to STOP IN YOUR TRACKS! In other words STOP before you do anything. Think about Jesus. Remember how He resisted His sin feelings for your sake. This is because YOU were more important to Him than His sin (**Luke 22:44**).

Are YOU willing to love Jesus more than you want to give into your sin? Stop, and remember what HE did for you (**Hebrews 12:2**). Are you willing to return just a portion of this love in return for His love for you? This is how you are to consider Jesus (**Hebrews 12:1-3**).

Then remember your Bible promise which was given to YOU (**Mark 4:14, 16**). Consider IT to be MORE IMPORTANT to YOU, than your SIN IS TO YOU. Ask Jesus for the strength to tell your sin "NO"!!! Then, determine in your mind that YOU WILL GET YOUR FRIEND his/her coffee with LOVE (**John 13:34, 15:12-13 & I Corinthians 13:1-3**)!! This means, you will be DETERMINED that you will get the coffee without complaining, because Jesus and your Bible promise means MORE to YOU, than your complaining means to YOU!!!

When you get to THIS POINT in your life, you are NOW DOING Jesus' Words, Jesus' gospel, God's law, God's Will and the "fruits of the Spirit" all at the SAME TIME!!! This is one of the ways you walk in the Spirit. And you do NOT fulfill the lust of your flesh!

> "This I say then, Walk in the Spirit, and ye shall NOT fulfill the lust of the flesh."

> **Galatians 5:16**

This is one of the ways in which you will be tested to see if you become offended and drop your promise or NOT. It depends on how deep you have rooted Jesus' Words and your promise down on the inside of your body, or NOT.

> "And these are they likewise which are sown on stony ground; who, when they have heard the word, immediately receive it with gladness;"

> **Mark 4:16**

Mark 4:16 is you hearing and receiving your Bible promise and believing it with all your heart. BUT, if you haven't studied and meditated on your promise to the point that it becomes ROOTED down into your heart and soul; when you are tested to see if you WILL do the "fruits of the Spirit", the law, God's Will, Jesus' Words and Jesus' gospel all at the SAME time, YOU WILL FALL into sinning because you will become offended with the test.

> "*__And have no root in themselves__*, and so endure but for a time: afterward, when affliction or persecution ariseth for the word's sake, immediately they are offended."

> **Mark 4:17**

Therefore, when your friend asked you to get him/her their coffee at the inconvenient time, Jesus' sacrifice, and your Bible promise are nowhere near your heart or mind. And the only thing which has interested you is how the favor has inconvenienced you. Thus, you will become offended and complain (**Mark 4:17**). When you complain, this sin takes away the credit of doing the "fruits of the Spirit".

> "But when the *__RIGHTEOUS turneth away from his righteousness__*, and committeth iniquity, and doeth according to all the abominations that the wicked man doeth, shall he live? *__All his righteousness that he hath done shall NOT be mentioned__*: in his trespass, that he hath trespassed, and in his sin that he hath sinned, in them shall he die."

> **Ezekiel 18:24**

"Know ye not, that to whom ye yield yourselves servants to obey, his servants ye are to whom ye obey; *whether of sin unto death*, or of obedience unto righteousness?"

Romans 6:16

You caused your deed of service and the "fruits of the Spirit" to be written by your name when you served your friend by getting him/her the coffee.

"Ye have not chosen me, but I have chosen you, and ordained you, that ye should go and bring forth fruit, . . ."

John 15:16A-C

"And I saw the dead, small and great, stand before God; and the BOOKS were opened: and another book was opened, which is the book of life: and *the dead were judged out of those things which were written in the books, according to their works.*"

Revelation 20:12

"For the Son man shall come in the gory of his Father with his angels; and then he SHALL REWARD *EVERY MAN* according to HIS WORKS".

Matthew 16:27

There is way too much scripture to copy in **Matthew 25:31-46**. But turn to the account and read it for yourself. When Jesus DOES return to this earth, He is going to JUDGE YOU as according to how YOU completed HIS Words on this earth. And it will be the CHRISTIANS who have REFUSED to bring forth the "fruits of the Spirit" and caused them to remain by their names, who end their lives in everlasting punishment!!

Now, let's return to our illustration. When you chose to complain about the inconvenient timetable, the fruit of the service remained by your name, BUT the credit of the "Good fruits of the Spirit" was removed (**Ezekiel 18:24** & **Romans 6:16**)!

> "Ye have not chosen me, but I have chosen you, and ordained you, that ye should go and bring forth fruit, and that your fruit should remain: . . ."

> **John 15:16A-E**

So, therefore, you CANNOT ask whatsoever you will and expect your prayer to be answered! You MUST cause your "good fruit of the Spirit" to remain by your name BEFORE God will answer your prayers!! This means, you must produce the "fruits of the Spirit" and have these fruits remain written by your name (**Revelation 20:12**). If you want the credit of doing these fruits to remain by your name, then you CANNOT allow any sin to flow from your mouth while you are doing the deed (**Ezekiel 18:24** & **Matthew 12:33-37**).

> "Ye have not chosen me, but I have chosen you, and ordained you that ye should go and bring forth fruit, and that your fruit should remain: . . ."

Why?

"... that whatsoever ye shall ask of the Father in my name, he may give it you."

John 15:16

This is completed by remembering Jesus and your PROMISE, and causing Jesus and your promise to be MORE important to you than your sin IS to you!! This is how you receive your promise and cause it to become ROOTED in your heart!! This is how you refuse to become offended and refuse to fall away from your Bible promise becoming manifested in your life. These are the types of tests, trials, persecutions, tribulations, afflictions and temptations Jesus is referring to when He tells us we will have trouble in our lives!!

He does NOT send sickness and disasters in our lives to test us. These adversities come as results of our own sins. For example, a child is abused because someone in the family sinned. This sin could have been a sin from a family member way back from a great, great, great, great grandfather or grandmother.

Remember, we are told in **Exodus 20:5** that our fathers' sins would be passed down from one generation to another. This sin can be passed down up to the fourth generation. And if there isn't someone who will turn from being faithful to family members, this snowball effect could start all over again and continue from generation to generation until someone in the family will turn to Jesus and pray for their loved ones (**Exodus 20:6**). The sin caused the curse of the sin to come into the family.

"As the bird by wandering, as swallow by flying, _so the curse causeless shall not come._"

Proverbs 26:2

"But it shall come to pass, if thou wilt <u>not</u> hearken unto the voice of the Lord thy God, to observe to do all his commandments and his statutes which I command thee this day; *that all these curses shall come upon thee, and overtake thee*:"

Deuteronomy 28:15

"And every one that heareth, these saying of mine, ***and doeth them NOT***, shall be likened unto a foolish man, which built his house upon the sand: And the rain descended, and the floods came, and the winds blew, and beat upon that house; and IT FELL: and GREAT WAS THE FALL OF IT."

Matthew 7:26-27

In other words, the people who refused to DO Jesus' Words in **Matthew 7:26-27** and God's commandments in **Deuteronomy 28:15** sinned (**John 12:48; 15:6** & **Acts 3:23**). And their sin of refusing to DO Jesus' Words and God's commandments allowed the world's curses to attack their families (**Matthew 7:27** & **Deuteronomy 28:15**).

If you don't understand the revelation knowledge revealed in this chapter, MEDITATE!! It will give you a NEW understanding of what sin does on the inside of a family. Sin calls for the curses. And if you refuse to do the Words which will reverse the curses; the curses will definitely attack you and your families!! Jesus tells us, YOUR FAMILY WILL FALL and great will be your failure!! The rain descending, the floods flowing and the winds blowing ***are the CURSES*** which occur in the families!! For example, abuse IS A CURSE!! This is WHY bad things happen in this world!! It IS

SIN and the refusal of DOING Jesus' Words (God's law) which allows disasters to occur in families (**Deuteronomy Ch. 28; Matthew 7:24-27** & **Luke 6:46-49**).

Remember, the curses are in the world. And our only protection is DOING Jesus' Words (**Psalm 91** & **Matthew 7:24-27**). They work for the people who will DO His Words (**Matthew 7:24-25**). And they DON'T WORK for the people who will NOT do His Words (**Matthew 7:26-27** & **Luke 6:46-49**).

Since the Holy Spirit is showing us how to come out from under the curses by DOING Jesus' Words in our lives, let Him show you another way to produce the "fruits of the Spirit" (or do Jesus' Words) in our next chapter.

CHAPTER 10

Doing The Fruits I

I N OUR LAST CHAPTER, the Holy Spirit showed us one of the ways in which we would be able to stop sinning. In this lesson He is going to show us another way we can stop. A few chapters ago, our precious Holy Spirit had said, doing the law causes us to stop sinning. He also said, doing the law and doing the "fruits of the Spirit" are one in the SAME actions. We already studied the fact that we MUST produce the "fruits of the Spirit" and cause credit of the fruits to remain by our names, if we want God to be able to answer our prayers (**John 15:16** & **James 4:1-3**).

So, why does Jesus necessitate doing the "fruits of the Spirit" to be able to receive our answered prayers? If we DO the "fruits of the Spirit" we will also be doing the law at the SAME time (**Matthew 7:12; 22:37-40; Luke 6:31; Galatians 5:14, 16, 22-23** & **I Corinthians 13:1-8**). Let the Holy Spirit explain this truth through His example of the fruits of love, meekness and temperance.

The "fruits of the Spirit" are love, joy, peace, longsuffering, gentleness, goodness, faith, meekness and temperance. In the last couple of chapters we were studying how to give the fruits of gentleness, goodness and love. Today, let's work on love, meekness and temperance! Temperance means: self-control. Meekness means: we have the right to fight back and stand up for our rights in a conflict, but we choose to give up our right to give mercy and kindness to another person.

For example: Jesus has all the RIGHT in the world to send us to hell if He wants to. We are the sinners, NOT JESUS (**Romans 3:23**)! HE did NOT SIN (**Hebrews 4:15**)! Therefore, we should be the ones who are destined for hell (**Romans 6:23**)!

But instead of telling US we must go to hell; Jesus gave up His right to condemn us (**John 3:18**). And, He went to hell for us on our behalf (**Isaiah Ch.53** & **Acts 2:25-27, 31**). He also has the RIGHT to curse us all, but He chose to give up His RIGHT and suffer the curse on our behalf (**Galatians 3:13**). This is how Jesus gave us our mercy, by using the fruit of meekness (**Luke 23:34**).

(In order for US to receive the full impact of Jesus' mercy which HE gave to US, we need to make Jesus' forgiveness personal. Yes, He died for the world, but He also died for us personally. IT WAS OUR SINS that put JESUS ON THE CROSS. Therefore, when HE said in **Luke 23:34** "Father, forgive them; for they know not what they do." Jesus was talking to God about US!!!) He gave US the mercy!!!

Now, our LORD and Master is looking at us, and telling us, we must deny our sin feelings and give the SAME mercy as He has given to us! This is what He completed in HIS LIFE for us (**Matthew Ch. 26-28; Mark Ch. 14-16; Luke Ch. 22-24;** & **John Ch. 18-21**!! So now, it is our turn to complete these steps in our lives for HIM (**John 10:1-5, 27; I Peter 2:21** & **I John 2:6**). This is HOW we are to follow after Jesus and DO in our lives for Him as He has done in HIS life for us (**Matthew 10:38** & **John 15:12-13**).

Mercy means: the power to forgive or be kind even though you know you were the one who was wronged (or sinned against). Forgiveness is the other WAY in which doing Jesus' Words, God's law, will cause us to STOP sinning!! You CANNOT resent and forgive at the same time! You either forgive totally, or your resentment will cancel out your fruits of meekness and kindness (**Ezekiel 18:24** & **Matthew 12:33-37**)!

This is a fight; the Holy Spirit knows this fact. This is why Jesus said you are to pick up your cross and fight your flesh in the same way in which He fought HIS (**Hebrews 12:1-4**)!! Your fight with your flesh (your sin) IS your cross you are to bear (**Matthew 10:38**)! Let's examine this from the Word.

> "And when he had called the people unto him with his disciples also, he said unto them, Whosoever will come after me, let him ***deny himself***, and ***take up his cross***, and follow me."

> **Mark 8:34**

Keep in mind, meekness is having the right to stand up for your rights. But you give up your right to allow another person to have what they think is theirs. For example: let's say you went to the grocery store. While you were shopping, you stopped in the middle of the aisle to do a price comparison for an item you need. But, an older gentleman also wants an item where you are standing. You were there first; therefore, you should have the right to finish your work and put up the item before he does. But, this man unexpectedly pushes you out of his way, picks up his article and leaves.

If you choose to follow in Jesus' footsteps, you are told to deny your feelings of resentment, (denying yourself) fight with your flesh feelings of revenge (put up your cross) and forgive the gentlemen as Jesus forgave us (and follow after Jesus) (**Matthew 16:24** & **Mark 8:34**).

But, it is up to YOU to make the choice. Are YOU going to give the fruit of meekness as was given to YOU (**Luke 23:34** & **Matthew 18:22-35**)? Or, are you going to resent the man for taking YOUR RIGHT away (**Galatians 5:15** & **Matthew 15:18-19**)? If you decide to give the meekness, then this act calls for you to forgive the man, get your item and move on (**Matthew 18:28-29** & **James 2:13**).

Remember: We were told, if we want the credit for doing the "fruits of the Spirit", than we must do them with LOVE in our hearts (**I Corinthians 13:1-3**).

> "And though I bestow all my goods to feed the poor, and though I give my body to be burned, *and have not charity, it profiteth me nothing*."

> **I Corinthians 13:3**

This is the *same* LOVE Paul is talking about in **I Corinthians 13:5**. So you could say: LOVE is NOT easily provoked!

> "Doth not behave itself unseemly, seeketh not her own, *is NOT easily provoked*, thinketh no evil;"

> **I Corinthians 13:5**

Take the time to think about what just happened to you. You were the ONE who had decided, "I am going to give the fruits of love, meekness and temperance". Hence, when the gentleman gave you the push, instead of becoming upset, it was the perfect time to use self-control over your anger. This would be using the fruit of temperance. This was the perfect time to use your meekness. You chose to FORGIVE the gentleman. And this was the perfect time to use the fruit of love. You determined in your mind, you WILL forgive the man with love in YOUR heart and NOT with resentment still lingering in the back of your mind and heart (**I Corinthians 13:1-8**).

There is no credit given to you for these fruits if you are resenting the fact that you had to give them (**John 15:16C**). You need to realize, if you are resenting, then this means you are still sinning (**Matthew 15:18-20**). Therefore, your sin has canceled out the "fruits of the Spirit" which you gave (**Ezekiel 18:21-24 & Matthew 12:33-37**).

In other words, let's say, you did decide to forgive the man (**Matthew 6:14-15**). This would be the GOOD FRUIT of mercy given to the man (**Matthew 7:19**). But later on, you told your friend what happened to you in the store; and you began to resent the gentleman all over again (**Matthew 15:18-20**).

This would be Jesus' Words taking effect on the inside of your body. He tells us in **Matthew 12:33** to cause all of our body to become totally good. Or else, the part of us which is bad will cause all of our body to become totally bad (**Isaiah 64:6 & Haggai 2:11-14**).

> "Either make the tree good, and his fruit good; or else make the tree corrupt, and his fruit corrupt: for the tree is known by his fruit."

> Matthew 12:33

This is WHY He tells us, as long as we let BOTH the GOOD fruits and the BAD fruits come out of the SAME body then, Jesus views us as being all bad. Our bad fruits are our bad feelings, thoughts and words (**Matthew 15:18-20 & Mark 7:20-23**).

"O generation of vipers, how can ye, being evil, speak good things? for out of the abundance of the heart the mouth speaketh."

Matthew 12:34

This is WHY your good fruits do NOT get the credit of being GOOD (**Isaiah 64:6**)! And this is WHY Paul called himself a wretched man in **Romans 7:24**.

The bad words, thoughts and feelings which come from the sin which still lives on the inside of you will come OUT of your mouth at some point and time (**Matthew 12:36**). You cannot stop your sin from coming out of your mouth. It WILL HAPPEN, whether YOU WANT it to or NOT! Jesus will cause what is in your heart to proceed out of your mouth when you are not even thinking about your actions (**Matthew 12:34; 15:18** & **Mark 7:20**). And when it does, Jesus sees you as having sin in your heart in abundance (**Matthew 12:33-34**).

You do NOT get the credit of doing the GOOD fruit because you didn't do the deed in LOVE, but resentment (**I Corinthians 13:1-3**). And this caused you to become the one who did *NOT* bring forth the GOOD fruit in **Matthew 7:19** & **12:33-34**.

When you do *NOT* produce the GOOD fruit, you end your life in the fire.

"Every tree that bringeth **NOT** forth *good fruit* is hewn down, and cast into the fire."

Matthew 7:19

Also, when you do NOT produce the GOOD fruit as Jesus has told you to do, this means you are NOT dwelling in Jesus (**John 15:1-6**). You must DO Jesus' Words in the physical, in your life, to be able to dwell (abide) in Jesus (**I John 3:24**). Look what happens to the person who refuses to abide in Jesus!

> "If a man ***abide NOT in me***, he is cast forth as a branch, and is withered; ***and men gather them, and cast them into the fire, and they are burned***."

John 15:6

This means **John 15:1-6** and **Matthew 7:19** agree with one another. They both tell you; you will end your life in the fire. Only **John 15:6** lets you know you will burn if you end your life in this fire!

Do you see the importance of studying your promise to the point that it becomes ROOTED down on the inside of you? When your promise becomes more important than resenting the man; giving out the fruits of love and meekness is easier to do. The Holy Spirit realizes some people may still have to fight their sin which lives in their hearts!

> "For the flesh lusteth against the Spirit, and the Spirit against the flesh: and these are contrary the one to the other: so that ye cannot do the things that ye would."

Galatians 5:17

The sin that resides on the inside of you will want to complain. It will want to be bitter. It will want to resent. Or it will want to rebel against Jesus' Words in any way it can (**II Corinthians 10: 4-6 & Galatians 5:17**).

But it is up to us to deny this rebellion and tell our sin "NO" (**Matthew 16:24; Mark 8: 34; II Corinthians 10:4-5: & Galatians 5:16; 23**). We are to tell ourselves: "We are going to give the fruit of meekness (forgiveness). And we are going to do it with the determination; WE WILL LOVE". This is so we can receive our credit of the "fruits of the Spirit" in heaven (**John 15:16 & 14:13**). And so we can receive our promise manifested (**Matthew 13:18-23; Mark 4:14-20 & Luke 8:11-15**). The gentleman, and our resentment of him, just isn't worth giving up our promise (**Matthew 10:38 & John 15:6-7**).

This explains why you CANNOT do Jesus' Words and sin at the SAME time. You will fight your sin and cast it down and out of your body so you can receive your credit (**Matthew 18:7-9; John 15:16C & Revelation 20:12**). Or your sin will cause you to do and say something which will take your credit away from your name (**Matthew 15:18-20; Mark 7:20-23; Ezekiel 18:24; Ecclesiastes 12:14; Matthew 12:33-37; 16:24-27 & Revelation 20:12**).

> "For by thy words thou shalt be justified, and by thy words thou shalt be condemned".

> **Matthew 12:37**

You cannot have it both ways. The "good" deeds you do, do NOT rid your body of its sin (**Matthew 12:33-37**). Thus, when the sin does come out of your mouth: then you are defiled (**Matthew 15:18-20; Mark 7:20-23 & Matthew 12:36-37**). This is WHY you NEED Jesus' instructions. And it is important for YOUR SAKE to follow them specifically.

> "Abide in me, and I in you. As the branch cannot bear fruit of itself, except it abide in the vine; no more can ye, except ye abide in me. I am the vine, ye are the branches: He that

abideth in me, and I in him, the same bringeth forth much fruit: *for without me ye can do NOTHING.*"

John 15:4-5

Matthew 18:7-9 will be explained better in the Holy Spirit's future lessons. But for now let's look at another way we can abide in Jesus' Words, in our next chapter.

CHAPTER 11

Doing the Fruits II

I N OUR LAST CHAPTER, we found out, we MUST abide in Jesus' Words by doing them, or we will end our lives in the fire to burn (**John 15:1-6**). So, here is another example of how we can abide in Jesus' Words. The Holy Spirit is going to teach us one of the ways in which we can do Jesus' Words from His lessons in **Matthew 7:12; Luke 6:31: John 13:34 & 15:12-13**. These scriptures are God's law all rolled up into one commandment (**Matthew 7:12; & Galatians 5:14**). They are NOT as hard to do as we may think. Let's look at our example.

You had decided on the inside of yourself that _you **were going to DO** the "fruits of the Spirit"_. This was so you **wouldn't** end your life in the fire to burn (**Matthew 7:19 & John 15:1-6**). Hence, God gave you two opportunities to do the "Spirit's fruits". The first person asked you for a cup of coffee when it didn't suit you. The second person pushed you out of his way so he could go first.

In the first situation: you chose to get the coffee, because you didn't have the heart to tell your friend, "No." But you did complain, because doing the service and complaining was just easier to do than telling your friend, "No, now isn't a good time to help you".

In the second incident, you hardly had a choice in the matter. The man came up, pushed you aside, and was gone just that quick. In both cases, you sowed the "fruits of the Spirit".

You gave your friend the fruit of goodness by getting the coffee. This means, you did the good deed of kindness by helping your friend. In the second event, you sowed the fruit of meekness when you gave up "your right" to select your item first. Both actions were sown! Subsequently, why wouldn't you be determined in your mind that you will do the deeds in LOVE so you can get the credit for doing the fruits (**John 15:16 & I Corinthians 13:1-8**)? You see, the deeds are still written by your name. It was just the credit of doing the "fruits of the Spirit" that were blotted off the books (**John 15:16E**).

You can get your credit back at any time. All you have to do is repent for resenting (**Ezekiel 18:21-22 & Matthew 12:33**). If you do, then YOU WILL BE DOING THE LAW OF GOD: because you will be doing the "fruits of the Spirit" with God's LOVE in your heart (**Matthew 7:12; John 13:34 & 15:12-13**).

You see, when you do the "fruits of the Spirit", you are sowing into another person's life the fruits of gentleness, goodness, meekness and LOVE. And if you WANT the credit for sowing these fruits, then they MUST be sown with the love, joy, peace, longsuffering, faith and temperance ***in your heart*** (**Deuteronomy 28:47; I Corinthians 13:1-8; & Galatians 5:22-26**)!!

Is it okay with you if people help you with resentment in their hearts? Or, wouldn't you want other people to help you with love, joy, peace, longsuffering, faith and self-control in their hearts? Guess what God's law is?

"Therefore all things whatsoever ye would that men should do to you, do ye even so to them; *for this is the law and the prophets*."

Matthew 7:12

"And as ye would that men should do to you, do ye also to them likewise."

Luke 6:31

"For all the law is fulfilled in one word, even in this; *Thou shalt love thy neighbour as thyself*."

Galatians 5:14

Meditate on this fact! This means, read **Matthew 7:12; Luke 6:31** & **Galatians 5:14, 22-23** again, again, again and again. God will give you the revelation of His law and the "fruits of the Spirit". When you DO Jesus' Words, God's law, and the "fruits of the Spirit" all rolled up into one service (**Galatians 5:14**), then you are "WALKING in the Spirit" (**Galatians 5:16**) and doing God's Will (**John 6:39-40**).

You see? Doing the law of God requires the very SAME actions as does the "fruits of the Spirit"!! When we start to do these actions with LOVE in our hearts, then this LOVE will replace our sin. And these acts of love will cause us to STOP sinning!!

This is NOT impossible to do.

"But Jesus beheld them, and said unto them, With men this is impossible; but with God all things are possible."

Matthew 19:26

"And Jesus looking upon them saith, With men it is impossible, but not with God: for with God all things are possible."

Mark 10:27

"For with God nothing shall be impossible."

Luke 1:37

"And he said, The things which are impossible with men are possible with God."

Luke 18:27

Jesus offers us His POWER to overcome our sin, if we *want it*! **Matthew 10:1; Mark 3:13-15** and **Luke 9:1** all tell us Jesus gives us His power over the devil and demons. This power includes overcoming the sin which rides on the inside of us.

The secret is; we *MUST want* this power; more than we *want our sin*!! The secret to wanting Jesus' POWER more than we want to sin is to find one of God's promises which will answer our prayers. And *WANT His promise* MORE than we *WANT to sin* (**Matthew 13:18-21; Mark 4:14-17;** & **Luke 8:11-13**). Once, we get to this point, we are well on our way to completing Jesus' Words and God's law!! Both are one in the SAME (**Deuteronomy 18:17-19** & **John 7:16-17**).

Look what Jesus says in **John 7:17.** He tells us, if we will DO *God's WILL* in our lives; then we will KNOW beyond a shadow of a doubt that doing Jesus' Words are the SAME actions as doing God's Words (**Deuteronomy 18:18** & **John 12:49-50**). When you do God's Words, you are doing God's law (**Deuteronomy 28:1-2** & **Ezekiel 18:21**).

Let's repeat this truth so it is not confusing. When you find out what God's WILL is and do it, then you are DOING Jesus' Words (**John 6: 39-40, 53-54, 56** & **I John 3:24**). When you do Jesus' Words in your life, then you are doing God's Words (**Deuteronomy 18:18; John 7:16-17** & **12: 49-50**). When you do God's Words then you are doing God's law (**Exodus Ch. 20;** & **Deuteronomy Ch. 6**). When you are doing God's law then you are doing the "fruits of the Spirit" (**Galatians 5:14-26**). When you are doing the "fruits of the Spirit" then you are walking in the Spirit (**Galatians 5:16**). So then, let's find out what God's _WILL_ is!!

> "Not every one that saith unto me, Lord, Lord, shall enter into the kingdom of heaven; *but he that doeth the _will_ of my Father which is in heaven.*"

> Matthew 7:21

We were just told by Jesus that we MUST DO *God's Will* (in our lives) before we can be allowed into heaven. God's Will is for us to be able to receive the everlasting life and be able to be raised up on the last day (**John 6:40**). We can receive everlasting life and can be raised up on the last day, if we DO Jesus' Words while we are living on this earth. Let's study this from the scriptures.

> "_And this is the Father's will_ which hath sent me, that of all which he hath given me I should lose nothing, but should

raise it up again at the last day. *And this is the **will** of him that sent me*, that every one which seeth the Son, and believeth on him, *may have everlasting life: and I will raise him up at the last day*."

John 6:39-40

What must we DO in order to receive and keep the everlasting life?

Do you remember the rich young ruler in **Matthew 19:16-22; Mark 10:17-22** and in **Luke 18:18-23**? He received the eternal life in his heart, because he DID God's law in the way which Jesus told him he MUST DO it (**Matthew 19:16-20; Mark 10:17-20** and **Luke 18:18-21**).

However, when Jesus told the young man the rest of the orders, which were required, in order for him to KEEP his eternal life, the young ruler couldn't commit (**Matthew 19:20-22; Mark 10:21-22 & Luke 18:21-23**). Therefore, he lost his eternal life which he had gained. So we can understand what Jesus told the young ruler, He repeats His Words in **John 6:53-54, 56**.

> "Then Jesus, said unto them, Verily, verily, I say unto you, Except ye eat the flesh of the Son of man, and drink his blood, ye have no life in you. Whoso eateth my flesh, and drinketh my blood, hath eternal life; and I will raise him up at the last day."

John 6:53-54

According to Jesus' Words in **John 6:53-54** we must eat our LORD'S flesh and drink His blood to be able to receive the everlasting life and to be able to keep it in our lives! So, how DO we eat Jesus' flesh and drink His blood?

> "He that eateth my flesh, and drinketh my blood, *dwelleth in me*, and I in him."

John 6:56

According to Jesus' Words in **John 6:56**, we eat Jesus' flesh and drink His blood by dwelling in Him. So how DO we dwell in Jesus? John gives us the answer in **I John 3:24**.

> "*And he that keepeth his commandments dwelleth in him*, and he in him. And hereby we know that he abideth in us, by the Spirit which he hath given us."

I John 3:24

So according to Jesus' Words in **John 6:39-40, 53-54, & 56** we do *God's Will* by dwelling in Jesus. And, according to John's words in **I John 3:24**, we *dwell in Jesus* by *DOING Jesus' Words*!! And again, when we DO Jesus' Words in our lives, we are DOING God's law, the "fruits of the Spirit", walking in the Spirit and *God's WILL all at the same time* (**Matthew 7:12, 21-23; 22:37-40; Luke 6:31; John 6:40, 53-54, 56; I John 3:24; John 7:16-17; 13:34; 15:12-13, 16; & Galatians 5:14, 16, 22-23**). Every one of these scriptures agree one with the other!!

In other words, we can know that Jesus abides in us by the "fruits of the Spirit" we do in our lives (**I John 3:24B**). This means we do the "fruits of the Spirit" with a good attitude whether it suits, or not (**Matthew 7:12; I John 3:24 & Galatians 5:14, 16, 22-23**). As a result, this is the way we are to DO Jesus' Words; Jesus' Gospel; God's Will; God's Law; the "fruits of the Spirit" and walking in the Spirit in our lives (**Matthew 7:21; John 6:40, 53, 54, 56 & I John 3:24**). According to Jesus' Words in **Matthew 7:21,** God' Will, God's law, Jesus' Words and the "fruits of the Spirit" must be completed by us, BEFORE we will be allowed into heaven. Thus, this is the proof that we MUST DO God's law before we are allowed into heaven! And before God will answer our prayers in the way we want Him to answer them (**John 9:31 & 15:16**)!

Proverbs is clear. Solomon tells us outright. If we CHOOSE to cover up our sins and leave them in our lives, *we will **never** prosper.*

> "He that covereth his sins shall NOT prosper: but whoso confesseth and ***forsaketh them*** shall have mercy."

> **Proverbs 28:13**

We MUST forsake our sins BEFORE God will allow us to prosper!

However, Jesus does tell us this is impossible to do, unless we abide in Him.

> "Abide in me, and I in you. As the branch cannot bear fruit of itself, except it abide in the vine; no more can ye, except ye abide in me. I am the vine, ye are the branches: He that abideth in me, and I in him, the same bringeth forth much fruit: ***for without me ye can do nothing.***"

> **John 15:4-5**

There are other ways in which we are commanded to abide in Jesus' Words. We will study some of them in the Holy Spirit's future lessons (**John 16:13-14**).

Since we must stop sinning if we want to live in heaven, the Holy Spirit is going to show us that we most definitely do have sins which we must overcome in the next chapter.

CHAPTER 12

The Rocky Heart I

I N THE HOLY SPIRIT'S previous chapters, we studied in **Joshua 1:8** and **Matthew 6:33** on how we are to meditate so we can plant our seed in our hearts. This would be doing **Matthew 13:18-19; Mark 4:14-15** and **Luke 8:11-12** in our lives. In Jesus' next lesson on "the parable of the sower", He talks about the rocky ground which is in our hearts. His teaching in **Matthew 13:20-21; Mark 4:16-17; Luke 8:13** is going to be lengthy, because it deals with men's sins. There is no easy way to deal with the sin which lives in our hearts. But it has to be done if we want God and Jesus to prosper us.

"He that covereth his sin shall **not** prosper: . . ."

Proverbs 28:13A

It also has to be done if we want to live in God and Jesus' Kingdom with Them (**John 8:34-35**). Remember, God doesn't allow our sin into heaven (**Revelation 21:27**). Thus, it is up to us to remove it from our bodies with our own free wills (**Luke 3:1-18**). These facts will be explained in detail throughout the rest of this book.

In the meantime, let's study the scriptures which tell us about our sin. I am sorry we are required to get into our own personal sins; but if

Jesus did this act, then it is up to us to do the same (**Matthew 19:21;**
Mark 10:21 & Luke 18:22). Reluctantly, let's begin.

We are told in **Romans 5:12** *all men* are born with *sin* in their
hearts.

> "Wherefore, as by one man *sin entered into the world*, and
> death by sin; and so death passed upon all men, for that *all*
> *have sinned*:"

> **Romans 5:12**

King David lets us know all newborn babies have sin in their hearts
from the womb.

> "*The wicked are estranged from the womb*: they go astray *as*
> *soon as they be born*, speaking lies."

> **Psalm 58:3**

And Jesus tells us in **John 8:44A** our father is Satan unless we
decide to change fathers. Just so you know; our father is Satan from
conception on. This means Satan becomes our father as soon as we
are conceived on the inside of our mother's womb.

> "Ye are of your father the devil, and the lusts of your father
> ye will do . . . ."

> **John 8:44A**

Note: There are some babies who accept Jesus from the womb.
Jeremiah was one of those babies (**Jeremiah 1:5**). And John the
Baptist was another (**Luke 1:41-44**). But even if we accept Jesus

from the womb, every human being has sin in their hearts (**Romans 3:23**). "For all have sinned, and come short of the glory of God."

This is **why** we need Jesus!!

Once we have sinned, we are doomed to be under the curses and then eventually death (**Ezekiel 18:20**). When we die without Jesus, we must then again suffer under the curses of hell (**John 3:36**). But, Jesus doesn't want us to live under these curses, so He gave us His words so we could be set free (**John 8:31-32**).

After we hear His words on salvation and we accept them into our hearts, we are set free from being *totally* doomed.

> "He that believeth on him is not condemned: but he that believeth not is condemned already, because he hath **_not believed_** in the name of the only begotten Son of God."

> **John 3:18**

However, accepting Jesus into our hearts does **not** automatically cause the sin we were born with to leave. Paul is proof of this fact. He tells us in **Romans 7:19-20** that the *evil things* he does **_not want to do_**, he does; and the **_good things_** he **_wants_** *to do*, he does **not do!**

> "For the good that I would I do not: but the evil which I would not, that I do."

> **Romans 7:19**

He then lets us know the evil things he does do is the *sin* that is still locked up on the inside of him.

"Now if I do that I would not, it is no more I that do it, *but sin that dwelleth in me."*

Romans 7:20

According to **Romans 7:20**, Paul again lets us know that even though people become born again (and they definitely are true believers, from the bottom of their hearts) (**Acts Ch. 9**), this experience will **not clear** the sin from their hearts.

Romans 6:16 agrees with **Romans 7:20**. It tells us we can either serve the sin which lives in our heart(s), or we can serve Jesus and His righteousness by doing what is right in Jesus' eyes. This verse is given to the born again believer. It is only the believers who are told to serve Jesus, because they are His servants (**John 12:26**).

"Know ye not, that to whom ye yield yourselves *servants* to obey, his servants ye are to whom ye obey; whether of sin unto death, or of obedience unto righteousness."

Romans 6:16

Jesus, Himself, lets us know we can be "born again" but continue to sin. He tells us in **John 8:34-35** that even though we live in God's house by being born again, if we refuse to stop serving our sin, we will be kicked out of His house. We serve our sin by sinning. This is being born again and still sinning.

"Jesus answered them, "Verily, verily, I say unto you, Whosoever committeth sin is the servant of sin. And the

servant abideth **not** in the house for ever: but the ___Son___
___abideth ever___."

John 8:34-35

Y'shua also tells about His bride in **Matthew 25:1-12**. Our Lord
calls His born again Christians "His BRIDE" in **Matthew 25:1**. He
tells us, His bride has become virgins because they have accepted
His blood to cover their sins (**Matthew 26:27-28**). Jesus definitely
considers all ten virgins to be a part of the bride of Christ because
He refers to all ten of them as waiting to marry the same bridegroom
(**Matthew 25:2-7**). Of course, this is the marriage of Jesus and His
Church (**Revelation 19:7**).

But there were ONLY five virgins who were smart enough to do
the work which brought sufficient oil to fill their lamps (**Matthew
25:2-9**). Read Jesus' Words. He tells us in **Matthew 25:3** the foolish
virgins took their lamps and did NOT take any extra oil with them.

> "They that were foolish took their lamps, ___and took NO oil___
> ___with them___:"

Matthew 25:3

The lamp which was given to each virgin is the Word of God.

> "___Thy word is a lamp___ unto my feet, and a light unto my
> path."

Psalm 119:105

"*For the commandment is a lamp*; and the law is light; and
reproofs of instruction are the way of life:"

Proverbs 6:23

This lamp (God's Words) was dropped into each of the virgins' hearts
when they became born again (**Jeremiah 31:31-33; Hebrews 10:12-16;
John Ch. 3; Matthew 26:26-28; Mark 14:22-24; & Luke 22:19-20**).

Take your concordance and look up the word oil. The anointing oil is
one of the most precious oils used. But, it is ***NOT free***. Just as Jesus
explains in **Matthew 25:1-9**; YOU must buy it with your own work
(**Matthew 25:9-10; Revelation 3:17-18; Matthew 25:9; Isaiah 55:1;
Matthew 13:44-46; Matthew Ch. 25 & John 15:16**). Read these
scriptures in the order as they were given and they will make sense.

The work which buys the oil is the work of doing Jesus' Words
(**Matthew 7:24-27; 25:31-46 & Luke 6:46-49**). It is the doing of
God's law (**Romans 2:13**). It is the doing of the "fruits of the Spirit"
(**Galatians 5:14-23**). It is the walking in the Spirit (**Galatians
5:14-16**). And it is the doing of God's Will (**Matthew 7:21; John
6:39-40; 53-56 & I John 3:24**) all rolled into the SAME action. This
is the work which causes you to STOP sinning and prepares you for
the Kingdom of God (**Ezekiel 18:21; Matthew 5:19-20; Luke 12:47
& Ephesians 5:26-27**). Remember? Jesus tells us in **Matthew 5:8** it
is only the PURE in heart who will see God (**Psalm 24:3-4**).

Doesn't God command us, in **Exodus 27:20**, that it is the PURE
oil which will cause the lamp to burn? And you cannot produce the
PURE oil unless you will first meditate. Doesn't Jesus tell us in
Matthew 6:33, the only way in which we are going to know God's
righteousness is by meditating first? When we meditate on God's
Words, the meditation causes His and Jesus' Words to work their

way down into our heart(s). Once Their Words become a part of us, we will do them!!

> "For as he thinketh in his heart, so is he: . . ."

Proverbs 23:7A

Once we do Jesus' Words, they will stop us from sinning and cause us to become pure (**Proverbs 19:16; Luke 10:25-28; 11:28; James 4:8-10 & I Peter 1:22**).

Jesus will NOT allow you to receive ANY of His oil unless you DO your own work. This is because NO one else can stop sinning for you. You are the ONE who has to DO your own changing (**Matthew 12:33-37 & I Corinthians 15:53-54**). So when the foolish virgins ask the wise to give them some of their oil, they were denied.

> "And the foolish said unto the wise, Give us of your oil; for our lamps are gone out. But the wise answered, saying, *Not so*; lest there be not enough for us and you: but go ye rather to them that SELL, and BUY for yourselves."

Matthew 25:8-9

Look what happens to the five foolish virgins!

> "And while they went to buy, the bridegroom came; and they that were ready went in with him to the marriage: and the DOOR WAS SHUT. Afterward came also the other virgins, saying, LORD, LORD, open to us. But he answered and said, *Verily I say unto you, I know you not.*"

Matthew 25:10-12

These virgins were definitely a part of Jesus' Church or they could have NOT been counted by Jesus as a part of the ten virgins who were going to marry Jesus in **Matthew 25:1**. But because they refused to DO Jesus' Words in their lives (**John 12:48** & **Acts 3:23**), they were left on the outside of God and Jesus' Kingdom (**Matthew 25:10-12**).

Also, because the five foolish virgins refused to do Jesus' Words they did NOT stop sinning (**Ezekiel 18:21** & **Matthew 12:33-37**). If they had completed **Ezekiel 18:21** & **Matthew 12:33** and caused their tree AND THEIR FRUIT to be good by stopping themselves from sinning, then this work would have prepared them for God and Jesus' Kingdom (**Luke 12:47**).

However, these foolish virgins told the people who were encouraging them to DO Jesus' Words in their lives "Leave me alone, I know what I am doing" (**Luke 12:45**)!

> "But and if that servant say in his heart, My lord delayeth his coming; and shall begin to beat the menservant and maidens, and to eat and drink, and to be drunken;"

> **Luke 12:45**

Jesus tells us in **Luke 12:46-47**, He doesn't take kindly to those words.

> "The lord of that servant will come in a day when he looketh not for him, and at an hour when he is NOT aware, and will cut him in sunder, and *__will appoint him his portion with the unbelievers.__*"

> **Luke 12:46**

In **Luke 12:46** our LORD tells us, He WILL return while His virgins are out doing what suits them. And He WILL give them their reward as according to the works they did while they were living on this earth!

> "For the Son of Man will come in the glory of His Father with His angels; and then *He WILL REWARD every man according to his works*."

> Matthew 16:27

This is according to the works each individual person did during his lifetime, NOT according to Jesus' works (**I Corinthians 3:9-15**). If you do NOT believe this truth, turn to **Matthew 25:31-46** and read how Jesus will reward His people! (This is just a note. The goats are the Christian people who bite and devour one another in **Galatians 5:15;** and the brethren who grudge one against another in **James 5:9**. The brethren are Jesus' Christians).

Therefore, according to Jesus' Words, these foolish virgins who did *NOT prepare themselves* for HIS RETURN will be given the SAME reward as the unbelievers will receive.

> "The lord of that servant will come in a day when he looketh not for him, and at an hour when he is not aware, and will cut him in sunder, *and will appoint him his portion with the unbelievers*. And that servant, *which knew his lord's will, and PREPARE NOT himself,* NEITHER DID ACCORDING TO HIS WILL, shall be beaten with many stripes."

> Luke 12:46-47

Again, this is the SAME words repeated in **Matthew 25:10-12**. The five foolish virgins are left on the outside of God and Jesus' Kingdom, to face the SAME punishment as the unbelievers must face.

> "And while they went to buy, the bridegroom came, and they that WERE READY went in with him to the marriage: ***and the door was shut***. Afterward came also the other virgins, sayings, LORD, LORD, open to us. But he answered and said, ***Verily, I say to you, I know you NOT***."

> **Matthew 25:10-12**

As was discussed before, this is NOT the only place where Jesus tells us; His church which will NOT do His Words will be left behind to face the Antichrist! Let's again look at our LORD'S Words in **Matthew 13:41-42**. But this time, with a much clearer understanding. He tells us, the people who are in His Kingdom and are still sinning from their flesh WILL BE REMOVED from His Kingdom and cast in the furnace of fire!

> "The Son of man shall send forth his angels, ***and they shall gather OUT of his kingdom*** all things that offend, and ***them which do iniquity***; And shall cast them into a furnace of fire: there shall be wailing and gnashing of teeth."

> **Matthew 13:41-42**

Jesus also tells us in **Matthew 7:21-23** that the people who are calling Him LORD and refuse to DO God's WILL (which is Jesus' Words and God's law) will also be left on the outside of His Kingdom.

> "Many will say to Me in that day, LORD, LORD, have we not prophesied in thy name? and in thy name have cast out

devils? and in thy name done many wonderful works? And then I will profess unto them, *I never knew you: depart from Me, ye that work inquity.*"

Matthew 7:22-23

You are reminded again; NO ONE can call Jesus LORD, unless they are saved by Him and they know the Holy Spirit!

"Wherefore I give you to understand, that NO man speaking by the Spirit of God calleth Jesus accursed: *and that no man can say that Jesus is the LORD, but by the Holy Ghost.*"

I Corinthians 12:3

"Jesus answered them, Verily, verily, I say unto you, Whosoever committeth sin is the servant of sin. And the servant abideth NOT in the house for ever: but the Son abideth ever."

John 8:34-35

The point is, unless you do Jesus' Words which cause you to stop sinning, you can be born again and still continue to sin. But as long as you continue to sin, you will NOT be allowed to stay in God's Kingdom forever!!

The Holy Spirit is impressing me to show you one more place where this truth is told.

"And Moses returned unto the Lord, and said, Oh, this people have sinned a great sin, and have made them gods of gold. Yet now, if thou wilt forgive their sin—; and if not, blot me, I pray thee, out of thy book which thou hast written. *And the Lord said unto Moses, <u>Whosoever hath sinned against me, HIM WILL I BLOT OUT of MY BOOK.</u>"*

Exodus 32:32-33

This statement agrees with Jesus' words in **Revelation 3:5;** in **Matthew 7:21-23; 8:11-12; 13:40-42; 25:1-12;** in **Luke 12:45-47;** in **John 8:34-35** and with Paul's words in **Romans 6:16, 23 & 7:20.** (These are just some scriptures which tell this truth).

If you do **not** clear the sin from your heart and **stop** sinning in this world, even though you are born again, you cannot **stay** in the book of life (**Exodus 32:31-33 & Revelation 3:5, 15-16**). And neither can you stay in God's Kingdom (**Matthew 13:40-42; 25:1-12 & John 8:34-35**).

Remember the man who didn't have the wedding garment on (**Matthew 22:11**)? This is the man who didn't do Jesus' Words. Thus, he didn't do the work to be able to earn the wedding garment (**Matthew 7:21; 16:27; 25:31-46; Luke 12:45-46; John 6:40, 53-54, 56; I John 3:24 & Revelation Ch. 2-3**). He wasn't allowed to stay at the wedding and marry Jesus because he was cast out into the outer darkness (**Matthew 22:11-13**).

We could go on and on with other scriptures, but the Holy Spirit is hoping that you are beginning to understand. If you don't do Jesus' Words now while you still have the opportunity to do so, the only chance you have left—is to face the Antichrist and stay faithful to Jesus (**Revelation Ch. 13**).

"*And it was given unto him to make war with the saints* and to overcome them: and power was given him over all kindreds, and tongues, and nations."

Revelation 13:7

These are **not** my words! They are GOD'S and JESUS'.

This is why Jesus teaches on the rocky ground in **Matthew 13:20-21; Mark 4:16-17** & **Luke 8:13**. This method is God and Jesus' way of clearing the sin from men and women's hearts. If you haven't guessed by now, the rocks are the sins that still live in our hearts, even after our "born again" experience.

We will look at **Matthew 13:20-21; Mark 4:16-17** and **Luke 8:13** in more detail in our next lesson.

CHAPTER 13

The Rocky Heart II

I N OUR LAST CHAPTER, the Holy Spirit proved to us, if we want to live with Jesus, we must do His Words (God's law) (**Deuteronomy 18:17-19 & John 12:48-50**). If we choose to ignore God's law (our Master's Words); we will be left on the outside of God and Jesus' Kingdom to be punished with the unbelievers (**Luke 12:45-47; John 12:48 & Acts 3:23**).

You see, if we refuse to do God's law (Jesus' Words), our sin(s) will remain on the inside of our bodies (**Matthew 5:19; 7:15-23; 13:40-41; & 12:33-34**). If our sins remain on the inside of us, we can't help it, we WILL do what our sin(s) want us to do (**John 8:21; 24; 34, 44; Romans 3:23 & 7:14-24**). As long as we continue to serve our sin(s) by sinning; Jesus cannot justify us because we are still sinning (**Matthew 7:19, 21-23; Luke 12:42-46; John 15:6 & I John 1:7**). If we are not justified by Jesus, we will not be able to live with Him (**Matthew 7:21-23 & 13:41**). Remember, we must stop sinning to be able to live with our Savior (**John 8:34-35**). There is only ONE WAY we can force ourselves to stop sinning, this is to make up our minds to do Jesus' Words.

You see, when we choose to do Jesus' Words, we are NOT sinning because we are doing what is right to do as according to God, Jesus, the Holy Spirit and the Bible Words.

> *"**Know ye not, that to whom ye yield yourselves servants to obey**, his servants ye are to whom ye obey; whether of sin unto death, **or of obedience unto righteousness**."*

Romans 6:16

In other words, when we are doing Jesus' Words we are serving the words of obedience. These words of obedience cause us to become righteous. This is how we put on Jesus' righteousness and become the righteousness of God (**Romans 3:20-22**).

But, when we choose NOT to do Jesus' Words, we are sinning because we are NOT doing the righteous Words. But we are doing the only other alternative we have to do, the words which are against Jesus' Words (**Matthew 12:25-31**).

They are against Jesus' Words because the only other words which are in the world are the world's words. The world's words are the words we have been taught since our birth. And they are from the tree of good and evil (**Genesis 3:1-6**). This is what makes the world's words the words of sin. They are totally in opposition to God's and Jesus' Words (**Isaiah 55:7-9** & **Ephesians 4:20-25**). And when we do the world's words instead of doing Jesus' Words we are in opposition to Jesus.

> "He that is not with me is against me; and he that gathereth not with me scattereth abroad."

Matthew 12:30

"Know ye not, that to whom ye yield yourselves servants to obey, his servants ye are to whom ye obey; whether of sin unto death, or of obedience unto righteousness.:"*

Romans 6:16

If we choose to refuse to do Jesus' Words because we want to live our lives in the way that we see it as being good, Jesus doesn't promise us success; *but failure*!!

"The way of a fool is right in his own eyes: but he that hearkeneth unto counsel is wise."

Proverbs 12:15

"And every one that heareth these sayings of mine, and doeth them not, shall be likened unto a foolish man, which built has house upon the sand: And the rain descended, and the floods came, and the winds blew, and beat upon that house **and it fell: and great was the fall of it.**"

Matthew 7:26-27

Not doing Jesus' Words is choosing to sin instead of choosing to do what is right. And sin always brings in the curses and failures. You see, because of sin, the curses are in the world (**Genesis Ch.3**). And they will attack anyone they can (**Deuteronomy 28:15-68**). They even tried to attack the vessels in heaven (**Hebrews 9:19-23**). This happened when Lucifer rebelled against God (**Isaiah 14:12-15**).

There is only one way we can stay entirely out from being under the curses which are raining down on this earth. Think of a rain storm. If you are standing outside while it is raining you are going to get wet, unless you use an umbrella. This is the way that it is with the curses which are in the world (**Genesis Ch. 3; Deuteronomy 28:15-68** & **Ephesians 6:12**). The curses are raining down from the clouds in the first heaven (**Ephesians 6:12**). The only way to protect ourselves from being attacked by them, is to stay under God's umbrella of protection by Doing Jesus' Words (**Matthew 7:24-25**).

God and Jesus are always trying to protect us. Therefore, even if we practice doing the evil, when we do perform the right words, we are protected by God. This is why the curses take a while to totally attack us. In other words, if we do well, then the curse doesn't attack. But if we do bad; then they do. Remember, what we sow, we must reap (**Galatians 6:7-8**). This is the way it was set up in the beginning (**Genesis Ch. 3** & **Deuteronomy Ch. 28**). And Jesus did NOT change the rules (**Matthew 5:17-19** & **Galatians 6:7-8**).

By refusing to do Jesus' Words in our lives, this refusal is causing us to sin (**Matthew 12:25-31** & **Romans 6:16**). As long as we continue to live our lives our way and in sin; Jesus' blood cannot cover our sins and protect us perfectly from the curses because He cannot go against the rules that were set in place long ago (**I Samuel Ch. 15; Proverbs 12:15; 14:12; 16:2, 25; 21:2; Matthew 7:24-27; 16:23-27; Luke 6:46-49; 12:42-46; 13:1-5; John 8:21, 24; 34-35; Galatians 6:7-8** & **I John 1:7**). There are nine different scriptures which all tell us the same warning. You need to take heed when scripture facts repeat more than one time (**Matthew 18:15-20**).

Thus, to stay away from the curses, we MUST do Jesus' Words. When we do; these righteous acts cause us to stop sinning (**John 15:1-3**). When we stop sinning is when Jesus can cover us with His blood; because, now He would not be breaking the original rules (**Galatians 6:7-8** & **I John 1:7**). This is when we can be justified, because He can cover our sins with His blood (**Romans 2:13**). Once we are justified, then the curses cannot attack us because they cannot attack an innocent person (**Galatians 3:13**).

> "As the bird by wandering, as the swallow by flying, so the curse causeless shall not come."

> **Proverbs 26:2**

Thus, it would be good for us to learn how to do Jesus' Words. So, the Holy Spirit is going to show us another way to do them in this chapter.

We have been studying Jesus' lesson on the "parable of the sower". If we can conquer this parable, we will be able to understand all of the other parables written.

> "And he said unto them, Know ye not this parable? And how then will ye know all parables?"

> **Mark 4:13**

So far we have come to the understanding that we must meditate on our Bible promises or the evil which is in this world has the RIGHT to rob our promises from us (**Matthew 13:10-19; Mark 4:10-15 & Luke 8:9-12**). As we studied in chapters 5 and 6 of this book, Satan does rob our promises if we refuse to meditate. He does have the right. And he uses this right because he knows if we ever get the revelation of how our promises help us, he has lost his grip on us.

But, once we have meditated and have started to plant our Bible promise down into our heart(s); this process has not removed our sin(s). In our last lesson we studied several scriptures which have proven this fact out to us. Once our promise is planted, if our sins are NOT removed from our bodies, they will cause our promise to die.

You see, Jesus compares the garden of our hearts to the farmer's garden. The farmer must till the hard ground of the field and plant his seeds into the soft soil. Meditation is the tilling of the soil and planting our seed (promise) into the field of our hearts.

But, if the farmer doesn't make sure that the rocks are removed from his field, the plants' roots will grow only until they hit the rocks, or rock, which is left in the ground. When this step happens, with a shallow root, the sun will cause the plant(s) to wither and die. If the sun doesn't kill the plant(s), then the storms will. The plant(s) cannot survive with a shallow root system.

This is the way it is with the garden of our hearts. The sin(s) (rocks) which are left in our hearts' soil will stop our promise's root from growing a deep root. Jesus proves this fact out to us in His lesson on the rocky ground. Like the farmer's field, our sins (rocks) must be removed from our body (bodies) if we want our promise to mature and manifest in the physical.

Let's study Jesus' Words from His lesson of the rocky ground from Matthew's account in **Matthew 13:20-21**. Jesus tells us in **Matthew 13:20** that we will hear His Words (promises), and when we first hear them they sound very promising to us.

> "But he that received the seed into stony places, the same is he that heareth the word, and anon with joy receiveth it."

> **Matthew 13:20**

We have already studied the fact; we MUST meditate so our seed (promise) can be planted. Thus, because we realize this fact, we do meditate and we do plant our promise. Nevertheless, even though we have meditated and planted our seed (promise) into our hearts, this meditation and planting did NOT remove the rocks (sins). So even though our plant has grown a root, it has hit one of our sin(s) (rocks) and has a shallow root system.

Again, like the farmer's garden, with a shallow root when the sun, high winds, hard rain, or floods hit the plant, these storms (hardships) will cause the seed (plant, promise) to wither and die.

Again, because Jesus' people do not understand the type of storms Jesus is referring to in **Matthew 7:24-27; 13:21; Mark 4:17; Luke 6:47-49 & 8:13** they lose their promises. The Bible Words are living Words. So, when the Christian loses their promise, there is no other place for the Words to live, but in the world. Thus, all the evil people have to do is to pick them up and use them wrongly. This is what happened to our prosperity.

Read Jesus' Words. He tells us in **Matthew 13:21** and in **Mark 4:17** the storms will be tribulation or persecution, or persecution or affliction. According to Webster's New World Dictionary, the word persecution means to keep on treating in a cruel way, especially for holding certain beliefs or ideas; harass. It doesn't say anything at all about the weather or disasters. When Jesus talks about the storms of life, He is talking about the way persecution will attack His people.

These are the types of storms He had to live under, and we are to live our lives as He lived His. Remember the rich, young, ruler? Jesus told him that the only other thing he had to do to be able to keep the eternal life is to live his life as Jesus lived His.

"Then Jesus beholding him loved him, and said unto him, ***One thing thou lackest***: go thy way, sell whatsoever thou hast, and give to the poor, and thou shalt have treasure in heaven: and ***come, take up the cross, and follow me.***"

Mark 10:21

Everybody thinks that Jesus was telling the rich, young, ruler to go and sell what he had, and give it to the poor, so that he would become poor also. This is not what Jesus was telling the young man. We do not have the time to go into this lesson. Jesus was NOT poor when He walked this earth. Remember the gold, frankincense and myrrh. These were not poor gifts. Jesus' family **did use** the money given to them. This is NOT why the young man walked away. He didn't want to be persecuted as Jesus was persecuted. Remember? Jesus told the rich, young, ruler to come and follow HIM, and live under the SAME persecution as Jesus was living under.

"Ye are they which have continued with me in my temptations."

Luke 22:28

"The disciple is NOT above his master, nor the servant above his lord."

Matthew 10:24

"Verily, verily, I say unto you, The servant is not greater than his lord; neither he that is sent greater than he that sent him."

John 13:16

"Remember the word that I said, unto you, The servant is not greater than his lord. If they have persecuted me, they will also persecute you; if they have kept my saying, they will keep yours also. But all these things will they do unto you for my name's sake, because they know not him that sent me."

John 15:20-21

The storms of life Jesus is referring to when He talks about storms is the persecution of believing Him and His Words. And the persecution you will live under when you actually do His Words in your life.

"Blessed are they which are persecuted for righteousness' sake: for theirs is the kingdom of heaven. Blessed are ye, *when* men shall revile you, and persecute you, and shall say all manner of evil against you falsely, for my sake. Rejoice, and be exceeding glad: for great is your reward in heaven: for so persecuted they the prophets which were before you."

Matthew 5:10-12

Notice, Jesus didn't tell us; these people may or may not persecute you. He said *when* they do. If you are one of the people who will follow Jesus, then you will be persecuted for doing so, in the same way as He was! The storms are the tribulation, the affliction and the temptation which goes on in our minds after we are persecuted. Jesus had to work with these SAME storms on the inside of Him.

"For we have not an high priest *which cannot be touched with the feeling of our infirmities*; but was in ALL points tempted like as we are, . . ."

Hebrews 4:15

Let's return to our scripture on the sower and study Jesus' Words from His viewpoint in our next lesson. In His lesson on the rocky ground, Y'shua shows us what happens to our promises if our rocks are not removed from our hearts.

CHAPTER 14

The Rocky Heart III

I N OUR LAST CHAPTER Jesus showed us another reason to meditate and to do His Words. In this lesson, He is going to show us what will happen to us if we ignore His Words in **Matthew 13:20-21; Mark 4:16-17** and **Luke 8:13.**

> "But he that received the seed into stony places, the same is he that heareth the word, and anon with joy receiveth it;"

> **Matthew 13:20**

Do you remember the lady who called the minister because her husband was abusing her, in chapter 6 of this book? She heard Jesus' Words (promise, seed) on her problem. She found a ministry who taught how to meditate. So, she went to the scriptures, and looked up all the words which taught her how to come out from under her abuse.

> "Oh that my people had hearkened unto me, and Israel had walked in my ways! I should soon have subdued their enemies, and turned my hand against their adversaries."

> **Psalm 81:13-14**

The meditation DID work, and life was improving again. This is **Matthew 13:21A; Mark 4:17A** and **Luke 8:13C** taking place in the lady's life. This is her enduring for the little while.

> "Yet hath he not root in himself, but dureth for a while: . . ."

> **Matthew 13:21A**

The seed was planted in the lady's heart. And the scriptures caused her husband to straighten up. This is the endurance and again, life was improving. But, the meditation did NOT remove the lady's rocks (sins) from her heart. So, the root from her promise was shallow because it hit one of the rocks, (sin(s) which she was born with).

Therefore, Jesus tells us in **Matthew 13:21; Mark 4:17 & Luke 8:13** that there is NOT enough root in the heart to last during her trial. You see, her husband had stopped abusing her because she was standing on God's Words by meditating on them. The evil cannot prevail against the scriptures (**Matthew 4:1-11 & Luke 4:1-13**).

But it can triumph over us when we fall into giving into our sins. And as long as we still have them on the inside of us, we will give into them and sin at some point in our lives. So again, we are told by Jesus in **Matthew 13:21 & Mark 4:17** that even though we have meditated and planted our seed and it has worked for a while; we still must be tested for the Word's sake.

> "Yet hath he not root in himself, but dureth for a while: *for when tribulation or persecution ariseth because of the word*, . . ."

> **Matthew 13:21A-B**

"And have no root in themselves, and so endure but for a time: *afterward, when affliction or persecution ariseth for the word's sake*, . . ."

Mark 4:17A-B

The persecution is done for the Word's sake because it deals with our sins. Think about what happens to you after you have been persecuted. Don't all kinds of feelings surface into your mind? You can't help it; you are offended when people hurt your feelings. This is what persecution is!! It is people going against the way you believe, or you see life as being right. For example: let's say the lady who meditated on the scriptures for her abusive husband, received a phone call from a lady friend. For clarification let's call the lady "Sue". The two ladies fell into a conversation on the scriptures Sue had been studying. The friend told Sue, she couldn't use scripture to stop her husband from abusing her. Sue knew better, because she was using her scripture to do that very thing. And it was working!

But Sue couldn't convince her friend that she knew what she was talking about and the two argued. They parted company on bad terms. Sue's husband came home and abused her the same evening. What happened?

"But he that received the seed into stony places, the same is he that heareth the word, and anon with joy receiveth it; Yet hath he not root in himself, but dureth for a while: for when tribulation or persecution ariseth because of the word, by and by he is offended."

Matthew 13:20-21

Sue had received her promise with joy in her heart (**Matthew 13:20**). And she was standing on her promise by meditating (**Matthew 13:19-21B**). She endured until she was tested with the phone call (**Matthew 13:18-21C**). When her friend offended (persecuted) her by going against the way she knew was right: Sue failed her test by becoming offended, and arguing back with her friend (**Matthew 13:18-21**).

There was not enough of Jesus' Words down on the inside of Sue to know how to stay out of the strife (the fight) (**Matthew 13:21A**). Strife (fighting) is sin (**Galatians 5:20**). And sin allows the curses to come down on top of us (**Deuteronomy Ch. 28; Matthew 7:24-27 & Luke 6:46-49**). Therefore, Sue's husband had the right to abuse her because she fell into the sin of strife during the day (**Deuteronomy 28:15, Matthew 5:19B; 26-27 & Luke 6:46, 49**).

Now, again, Sue has to fight with her own emotions. She wants to convince her friend, she is right. She wants to become mad at God and the scriptures. She is angry and hurt because her husband abused her again. And she certainly doesn't know what she did that was so wrong. Her meditation worked before, why isn't working now? She is asking what went so wrong. The Lord is NOT going to answer her question because she would become offended at His answer (**Isaiah 57:15-21**).

Her next emotion (feeling) would be; if what I am doing is NOT working, why even try? Maybe, my friend is right? Maybe meditating on the scriptures doesn't help. This is her temptation to fall away from her promise.

> "They on the rock are they, which, when they hear, receive the word with joy; and these have no root, which for a while believe, and in time of temptation, fall away."

> **Luke 8:13**

Are you beginning to see how our rocks (sins) can kill our promise? All the emotions (feelings) which surfaced into Sue's mind are our sin feelings!! And these feelings can drown out our promise because they will take over our minds.

Our thoughts are on our own feelings and on how we want to prove ourselves to be the ones who are right. These thoughts are our rain that is raining down into our hearts and minds. And the rain of all our thoughts is drowning out the root of our promise (**Matthew 7:27**). What are we concentrating on, our promise, or how we want to make things right for us (**Matthew 16:24-27**)? God will not answer these kinds of thoughts because they are sin.

Our thoughts would be, "How could these feelings be sin?" We are the innocent ones here. All we are doing is defending ourselves. These are the kinds of thoughts (winds) which fight against our minds. They are the tribulations which fight against our promise. If we allow these winds (thoughts) to continue in our minds, the winds (thoughts) will eventually defeat the promise from God. We are more concerned with defending ourselves, then we are in defending our promise. If we don't calm down and allow the Holy Spirit to explain to us how these feelings are sin, our pride will take over and wither our promise and it will totally die (**John 15:1-6**).

To defend yourself is always SIN because it is trying to exalt your feelings over others (**Luke 18:10-14**).

> "I tell you, this man went down to his house justified rather than the other; for every one that exalteth himself shall be abased; and he that humbleth himself shall be exalted."

> **Luke 18:14**

Jesus tells us, we are NOT allowed to defend ourselves when we have been offended. He was offended all during His life. But, He prayed that God would give Him the strength to stay out of the sin of defending Himself (**Hebrews 5:7**). And we are told to follow in His footsteps by doing as He did for us.

"He that saith he abideth in him ought himself also so to walk, even as he walked."

John 2:6

"And when he had called the people unto him with his disciples also, he said unto them, Whosoever will come after me, let him DENY himself, and take up his cross, and follow me."

Mark 8:34

The denying of yourself is the fact that you are not allowed to defend yourself when you are confronted. Jesus wasn't allowed to defend Himself, therefore, we are NOT allowed to defend ourselves, either. **Matthew 12:10-14, 22-31** are two places where Jesus was persecuted for His beliefs. **Mark 5:21-40 & 6:1-6** are two others. **Luke 4:15-30** is another. **John 9:1-34** is another. Jesus was NOT allowed to defend Himself in any of these places. If we are to follow in His footsteps, then NO, we are NOT allowed to defend ourselves, either. We are told to deny our feelings of infirmities and just walk away from our accusers.

Why would we want to walk away from a fight and not confront our accusers? For one, strife (fighting) is sin. And once we sin, the curse has a right to attack us. Secondly, the only Words which close the mouth of accusers is the scriptures (**Matthew 4:1-11**). And unless we know as much scripture as Jesus, we do NOT have the ammunition to confront our foes. Thirdly, Jesus has commanded us to give out the "fruits of the Spirit". And meekness is one of the fruits. This means, you are to give the mercy and forgiveness to others as Jesus gave it to us (**Luke 23:34**). This means, you walk away and let the others be right, whether they are right or not. This is how you give the mercy (**Luke 4:15-30** & **Galatians 5:23**). And we are to do it whether the other person deserves the forgiveness or not (**Matthew 6:14-15**). Fourthly, this is NOT the reason Jesus wanted us to be persecuted.

He wants us to be persecuted because He wants our sin feelings to rise to our minds. He wants this to happen so that we can confess our feelings to Him. He wants us to tell Him how we are feeling, but NOT in a complaining attitude. Complaining and murmuring is sin (**Numbers 14:1-12** & **Jude 10-16**). But He wants us to tell Him in a humble confessing attitude (**Isaiah 57:15**). This is the first step of eliminating our sins (**Psalm 51** & **I John 1:9**).

Let's return to Sue. When the phone call came in, He wanted her to take the call. But when the two ladies fell into the conversation about the scriptures, He wanted her to listen to the accusation, become offended, but tell her foe, "I am sorry, I just cannot answer you at this time." And hang up the phone.

Then He wanted Sue to go to Him, and confess to Him the feelings she was feeling because of the accusation. This is why Jesus tells us that the persecution is given to us for the Word's sake. If we will follow through with Jesus' instructions, these instructions will clear the sin from our hearts (**John 15:1-3**). And then we will NOT be tempted to sin, because our sin will be dead (**Romans 6:6**).

"For he that is dead is freed from sin."

Romans 6:7

Once we learn how to crucify our sins, Jesus not only can justify us, but, He can allow us to prosper!!

"He that covereth his sins shall NOT prosper: but whoso confesseth ***and forsaketh*** them shall have mercy."

Proverbs 28:13

Proverbs 28:13 tells us we not only must confess our sins to Jesus to be able to ***receive the mercy, but we must also forsake them as well.*** So we will study **Proverbs 28:13** in more detail in our next lesson.

CHAPTER 15

The Just Man

I N OUR LAST THREE chapters, we were told by Jesus in **Matthew 13:20-21**; in **Mark 4:16-17**; and **in Luke 8:13** our sins (rocks) have **not** been removed from our hearts even though we are "born again". We also found out in **Romans 7:14-24** and in **John 8:34** we can be saved and STILL sin. Consequently, if we refuse to do God's law which causes us to STOP sinning, then Jesus CANNOT justify us because we are still sinning (**Romans 2:13 & Matthew 12:33-37**).

Moreover, we read in **Matthew 13:40-42 & 25:1-12** if we want to be able to stay in God and Jesus' Kingdom, then we *must* forsake our sins (**Luke 12:45-47**). This also *must* be done if we want God's prosperity (**Proverbs 28:13**).

Since we are studying how to receive "God's Prosperity", it would be good to know what our requirements are in order to receive it. Solomon tells us in Proverbs: You *must* be considered by God and Jesus to be the "JUST" man to be able to receive our LORD'S prosperity.

"A good man leaveth an inheritance to his children's children: and *the wealth of the sinner is laid up for the JUST.*"

Proverbs 13:22

Did you notice the transfer? God takes the sinner's wealth and gives it to the "JUST" man! The church people are not worried about this statement. They have the idea that God and Jesus consider the "church" to be the "JUST" people. The Christians have this idea, because they have been taught Jesus' blood covers their sins. Therefore, it doesn't matter what they do in their lives, they consider themselves to be the *"just people"*, because of Jesus' blood.

But it doesn't work this way. God and Jesus do NOT consider us to be the "JUST" people until we conquer our sins. Let the Holy Spirit explain.

We need to look at reality. Can you honestly say *all* Christians are wealthy? If you are truthful with yourself, you must answer "NO"! You and I both know most Christians are struggling when it comes to finances. A good way to consider this truth: "Are YOU personally wealthy?" In other words, do you have the sinner's wealth in *your hands*?

James tells us in **James 5:1-3** God and Jesus plan on transferring the sinner's wealth to us in the last days.

> "Go to now, ye rich men, weep and howl for your miseries that shall come upon you. Your riches are corrupted, and your garments are motheaten. Your gold and silver is cankered; and the rust of them shall be a witness against you, and shall eat your flesh as it were fire. *Ye have heaped treasure together for the last days.*"

> **James 5:1-3**

Most of us realize we are living in the last days. So, the timetable is now. Subsequently, if we are to be considered the "JUST" people, WHY hasn't the transfer taken place yet?

There has to be a reason WHY God hasn't helped us financially!

Read **Proverbs 28:13** with your spiritual eyes open to the Holy Spirit.

> "He that *__covereth his sins shall NOT prosper__*: but whoso confesseth and *__forsaketh them__* shall have mercy."

> **Proverbs 28:13**

We not only MUST confess our sins, BUT we MUST also FORSAKE them to be considered by God and Jesus to be the "JUST" man.

For the people who claim that this is the Old Testament teaching and **Proverbs 28:13** doesn't apply to today's Christians; you need to know—Jesus agrees with this scripture!

Let's study this truth from the New Testament.

Because we have sinned, we MUST be justified by Jesus to become the "JUST" person. The Webster's New World Dictionary defines the word justify; "as to show to be right or fair, or to be free from blame or guilt".

Our LORD tells us in **Matthew 7:21-23** that we MUST do *God's Will* in our lives or we CANNOT enter into heaven. In other words, Jesus is telling us in His lesson, if we refuse to DO *God's Will*, which is God's law, than we will NOT be justified by our LORD. If we were justified by Y'shua, then He would NOT tell the people who have refused to do God's Will, (God's law) ". . . *I never knew you: depart from me, ye that work iniquity*" (Matthew 7:23B).

Accordingly, if Jesus calls the person who refuses to do God's Will, the man who works iniquity, does this sound like the person who is free from blame or guilt? It only makes sense that we MUST do *God's WILL*, (God's law), to be able to be justified by Jesus (**Romans 2:13**) and to be called the "JUST" man in **Proverbs 13:22**.

Jesus says in **Matthew 13:40-42** as long as we are continuing to sin, we are offending God, Jesus, the Holy Spirit, and the people around us. Therefore, when Y'shua does return to this earth, instead of justifying us and taking us to heaven, He will cast us into the furnace of fire.

John tells us in **I John 1:7** we MUST walk in this world in the SAME way Jesus is in the light—or Jesus' blood will NOT cover our sins!! Jesus is in the light without the sin (**Hebrews 9:28**). Therefore we must walk in this world WITHOUT the sin, or again, Jesus WILL NOT cover our sins with His blood. Consequently, if our sins are NOT covered by Jesus' blood, then we are not free from our blame and guilt.

Does this sound to you as if Jesus considers us to be the "JUST" man? Catch the revelation people! Jesus doesn't consider us to be the "JUST" man unless we decide to do God's law! Doing God's law, (Jesus' Words), causes us to forsake our sins! **Proverbs 28:13** can and DOES apply to the "born again" believer of the New Testament!!

Matthew 8:11-12; 25:1-12, 31-46; Mark 8:33-38; 9:38-50; Luke 12:41-48; 16:1-13; John 6:39-58; I John 3:24; John 15:1-6 and **Revelation 3:15-16** are just a few places where Jesus tells us that He does NOT set us free from our blame or guilt, unless we do God's law.

It would take the rest of this book to prove this fact out to you. And, this is NOT what we are studying. We are studying the requirements which are required in our lives to be able to receive "God's Prosperity". And being able to be the "JUST" man is one of the MAIN requirements which are needed (**Proverbs 13:22 & 28:13**)! Therefore, it was compulsory to find out why Jesus doesn't consider us the "JUST" man. We must do God's law before, Jesus will consider us to become "JUST" (**Romans 2:13 & Matthew 7:21-23**)!!

I cannot stress to you enough: Y'shua will return to this earth! He will judge all of us! If you do not turn from your WAYS and do Jesus' Words, you will be left behind to be judged with the unbelievers (**Matthew 25:1-12 & Luke 12:45-47**). Therefore, instead of being justified by Jesus and receiving the wealth of the sinner (**Proverbs 28:13**), you will just be a part of the sinners' punishment (**II Thessalonians 1:7-9**)!!

We must forsake our sins, before we can be justified (**Proverbs 28:13 & Matthew 7:19, 21-23; 13:40-42; John 8:34-35; 15:1-6, 16; I John 1:7 & Romans 2:13**)!

So, in the rest of this book, the Holy Spirit is going to show us how we are to forsake our sins. ☺

CHAPTER 16

Bitter Words

IN OUR LAST CHAPTER we were told we must forsake our sins if we want to prosper (**Proverbs 28:13**). But, if we don't recognize our OWN sins, or see how we are immoral, then it is hard for us to forsake sins we don't realize we are doing!! So, God and Jesus have created three different ways to reveal our sins to us. The first is to confront us directly by having our sin told to us by an individual. Although it doesn't seem like it at the time, this person really is commissioned by God to tell us of a sin we have committed against God, Jesus, the Holy Spirit, this person or other people.

> "Moreover if thy brother shall trespass against thee, go and tell him his fault between thee and him alone: if he shall hear thee, thou hast gained thy brother."

> **Matthew 18:15**

Even though the faultfinder is commissioned by God, most people get highly offended when they are corrected directly. And they will let their accuser know just how irritated they are with the allegation. As a rule, the corrected person's irritation will cause the confronter to also become upset, and this situation can cause both people to become offended with one another. Now, both persons have a problem they must overcome.

"***But if he will NOT hear thee***, then take with thee one or two more, that in the mouth of two or three witnesses every word may be established."

Matthew 18:16

Most of the time, **Matthew 18:16,** is ignored by the person who has done the correcting. He/she just becomes upset with the rejection.

The person, who was corrected, was offended at the harsh and bitter words of being told he/she had sinned. And the second person, who did the correcting that was NOT received and was told how wrong they were, has to overcome the harsh, bitter words and the rough treatment given to him/her. This becomes a frustration in the relationship between both individuals.

What did John tell us we MUST do before Jesus would cleanse us from our sins?

"But if we walk in the light, as he is in the light, ***we have fellowship one with another***, and the blood of Jesus Christ his Son cleanseth us from all sin."

I John 1:7

We MUST have a real relationship with ONE ANOTHER. We cannot be true friends with each other when we are secretly upset with the other person. The words we speak out of our mouth(s) about the other person will let us know if we are still holding a grudge or NOT!

"But I say unto you, That every idle word that men shall speak, they shall give account thereof in the day of judgment. For by thy words thou shalt be justified, and by thy words thou shalt be condemned."

Matthew 12:36-37

We must HAVE a GOOD relationship with each other from our **own hearts (I John 1:7)**. God, Jesus, the Holy Spirit, and all the angels who are assigned to us personally; Satan and all his demons who are allotted to us personally; and all the people we know can read our heart(s). Jesus tells us, this *cloud of witnesses* can distinguish what is on the inside of our heart(s) by the words which come out of our mouths (**Matthew 7:15-20; 12:33-37; 15:18-20; Mark 7:18-23; & Luke 6:43-46**). It is the *WORDS, which come out of our mouths which will defile us*.

> *"But those things which proceed out of the mouth come forth from the heart; and they defile the man."*

Matthew 15:18

> **"For by thy words thou shalt be justified, and by thy words thou shalt be condemned."**

Matthew 12:37

> *"Wherefore seeing we also are compassed about with so great a cloud of witnesses*, let us lay aside every weight, and the sin which doth so easily beset us, and let us run with patience the race that is set before us,"

Hebrews 12:1

We have to make things RIGHT from our OWN heart(s), NOT by the other person's. Thus, for the person who was corrected, the Holy Spirit is talking to YOU personally. You must examine yourself, and find out WHY your accuser was sent to you (**Matthew 18:15**).

> "*But let a man examine himself,* and so let him eat of that bread, and drink of that cup."

I Corinthians 11:28

You must go to God humbly and ask Him if your accuser was right in anything said. If you will come down off of your anger (and pride) at the accusation, God will answer you. But if you go to God while you are still angry, because you feel as though you have been accused falsely, then God will NOT answer your question!! You need to know, God WILL NOT **answer sin (Isaiah 59:1-3)**. You also need to know, your anger to defend (justify) yourself is always sin (**Luke 18:9-14**).

> "I tell you, this man went down to his house justified rather than the other: for every one that exalteth himself shall be abased; and he that humbleth himself shall be exalted."

Luke 18:14

If the Holy Spirit lets you know that there is sin attached to the accusation, then it is up to you to repent and forgive your accuser (**Luke 13:1-5: I Corinthians 11:24-30 & Matthew 6:14-15**).

To "repent" means: we must make a 180 degrees change. Meaning: we HAVE to change our thinking around and realize we MUST stop sinning. This means we must stop doing any part of the sin, in which we were charged with. We must think about the way we were accused! Did we do anything wrong? We must be aware of our own sin and realize what we are doing to ourselves and the other people who are in our lives.

> "I acknowledged my sin unto thee, and mine iniquity have I not hid. I said, I will confess my transgressions unto the LORD; and thou forgavest the iniquity of my sin."

Psalms 32:5

But, if you are innocent—then praise God and forgive your accuser!

Now that the Holy Spirit has dealt with the person who was accused of sinning, He will deal with the person who was rejected. Let's refresh by reading our scripture again.

> "Moreover if thy brother shall trespass against thee, go and tell him his fault between thee and him alone: if he shall hear thee, thou hast gained thy brother."

Matthew 18:15

More often than not, the accuser is NOT received; and is treated harshly with bitter words in return for the allegation. Or if, no words were said, the accuser is more than likely held in contempt by the accused person.

For the confronter, you need to know; **I John 1:7** applies to you as well! You cannot hold a grudge just because you were rejected.

> "But if we walk in the light, as he is in the light, *we have fellowship one with another*, and the blood of Jesus Christ his Son cleanseth us from all sin."

I John 1:7

To be in good fellowship with one another, you must forgive your offender Jesus' way before Jesus' blood can cleanse you from your sin(s). Holding a grudge is sin (**Leviticus 19:18**)!

> *"Grudge not one against another, brethren, lest ye be condemned*: behold, the judge standeth before the door."

James 5:9

This is ONE form of the bitter words which exist in the Christian world. There are all kinds of astringent (cutting, biting) words and arguments which occur among the Christians. The bitter words and arguments can go from two believers disagreeing about their beliefs; to big churches splitting in two, to form new churches. The bitter words and arguments are present in different families and in all the different nations throughout the world. As a matter of fact, this is how wars originate!

> *"From whence come wars and fightings among you?* come they not hence, even of your lusts that war in your members?"

James 4:1

Many times we go out in public and are treated rudely and we become offended with the way we have been treated. To put it bluntly, any time we are offended, it is because we are treated rudely. Or, it is because astringed words have come against us.

Did you know Jesus came to this world to send this rude treatment and bitter words against YOU? In other words, Jesus came to this world to make sure you are offended.

"Think not that I am come to send peace on earth: *I came NOT to send peace, but a sword*."

Matthew 10:34

The *sword is the bitter words* which cause us to become offended.

"*Who whet their tongue like a sword*, and bend their bows to shoot their arrows, *even bitter words*:"

Psalm 64:3

Why would Jesus come to this earth to send the bitter words (the sword) to us? Why does He want us to become offended?

Remember what we are studying? Jesus is trying to get us to recognize our sins! Therefore, if He cannot send a person to us directly to get us to acknowledge our sins, then He will send the sword (bitter words) against us to offend us. This is to cause our offensive feelings (and the sin of becoming offended) to come from inside of our hearts to the surface of our minds! This is so we will recognize the sin feelings which are bottled up on the inside of our heart(s).

This is the second way in which Jesus wants to reveal our sins to us!

Our Savior offended the Pharisees all the time. **Matthew 15:1-12** is just one place in Jesus' Gospel where He offended the Rabbis. He was hoping these men would realize why He was offending them. Our LORD wanted them to see that He was offending their sinful ways, and not them personally (**Matthew 12:1-8, 9-14 & 15:1-14**). And He wanted them to change their minds about the way they were thinking (**Isaiah 55:7-11**). It worked for some (**John 3:1-21**). But most of the Pharisees just became offended and sought ways to get rid of their antagonist (**Matthew 12:1-14** & **Mark 3:1-6**).

Our LORD is not with us today, so He (Himself) cannot offend us. However, He has sent other people to us who do not mind offending others! ☺ This is to cause us to become offended so our defensive feelings will surface into our minds (**Matthew Ch. 18**).

> "Woe unto the world because of offences! for it must needs be that offences come; but woe to that man by whom the offence cometh! Wherefore if thy hand or thy foot offend thee, cut them off, and cast them from thee: it is better for thee to enter into life halt or maimed, rather than having two hands or two feet to be cast into everlasting fire. And if thine eye offend thee, pluck it out, and cast it from thee: it is better for thee to enter into life with one eye, rather than have two eyes to be cast into hell fire. Take heed that ye despise not one of these little ones; for I say unto you, That in heaven their angels do always behold the face of my Father which is in heaven."

Matthew 18:7-10

Because it will take too long to explain Jesus' intent, we will close for now and pick up with His lesson on this scripture in our next couple of chapters.

CHAPTER 17

Our Flesh

BEFORE THE HOLY SPIRIT even starts this lesson, He has impressed me to go into the different ways people become offended. One of the main and most obvious ways we can become offended is when people offend our "flesh" feelings.

Some examples are: people can accuse us of sinning. They can refuse to cooperate with the things WE WANT to do. They can treat us with disrespect. They can say hateful, mean words which they know will hurt our heart(s). They can persecute us by ignoring us. They can be rude in stores and elsewhere. They can refuse to be a good team worker. Our bosses (or co-workers) can be unfair in the amount of work they put on us. And the list can go on and on.

<u>You</u> can offend other people as well. Many times, you are NOT aware that YOU are the one doing the offending. Your attitude of being snobbish and/or unforgiving is very offensive to God, Jesus, the Holy Spirit and the person receiving your bad attitude (**Exodus 32:9-10; Isaiah 48:4; & Matthew 9:11-13**).

You offend God, Jesus, the Holy Spirit and some people when you give into your sin (**Exodus 32:31-35; Matthew 13:41; 25:31-46; Mark 7:15-23; Luke 12:45-48; 16:1-13 & Revelation Ch. 2-3**). You offend Them when you refuse to be corrected (**Matthew 18:15-17 &**

Hebrews Ch. 12). You offend Them when you fight against Jesus' truth (**John 12: 48** & **II Corinthians 10:4-6**). And you also offend Them and yourself when you fight your own God-given Spirit (your conscience) (**John 3:6, 19-21;** & **Galatians 5:17**).

Let's back up for a few minutes and do some explaining. When we were born, we came into this world with two parts. We were born with our soul(s) and our body (bodies).

> "And the LORD God *formed man of the dust of the ground*, and breathed into his nostrils the breath of life; and man became a *living soul*."

> **Genesis 2:7**

God made Adam with a body and a soul that was totally good. He served God with all his heart, all his soul, and with his entire mind.

> "Jesus said unto him, Thou shalt love the LORD thy God *with **all** thy heart*, and *with **all** thy soul*, and *with **all** thy mind*."

> **Matthew 22:37**

But when Adam gave his heart, his soul, and his mind over to Satan, his mind, heart and soul changed from being all good to being good and bad (corrupt). This is the tree of knowing the GOOD and the EVIL (**Genesis 3:5**).

> "Either make the tree good, and his fruit good; or else make the tree corrupt, and his fruit corrupt: for the tree is known by his fruit. O generation of vipers, how can ye, being evil,

speak good things? for out of the abundance of the heart
the mouth speaketh."

Matthew 12:33-34

And now because of Adam's sin, this "sin" has been passed down to
all of us.

"Wherefore, as by one man sin entered into the world, and
death by sin; and so death passed upon all men, for that all
have sinned:"

Romans 5:12

This is the same spirit which exists in the world (**John 8:44**). We
also cannot help the fact that Satan's spirit lives on the inside of us.
We were born with his sin already existing on the inside of our bodies.
Because our soul(s) belong to Satan, Jesus calls this spirit our "flesh"
(**John 1:13; 3:6 & 8:44**).

Remember, we were born with two parts, our body and our soul. We
know our body because we use it daily. But the inside of us is a little
more difficult to detect. It is this inside part of our body Jesus calls
"flesh".

"That which is born of the flesh is flesh; . . ."

John 3:6A

Our soul lives on the inside of our body. Our soul is made up of
our mind, our feelings and our will. Our mind, feelings and will are
our personality. Our personality is in the center of our being. This
is WHY Jesus calls our soul(s) "our heart(s)" (**Matthew 15:17-20**

& **Mark 7:20-23**). Before we accepted Jesus into our lives, we lived as according to how our minds, our sin feelings and our wills (our personalities) saw fit.

> "There is a way which seemeth right unto a man, but the end thereof are the ways of death."

Proverbs 14:12

Most of the time, our actions would be against Jesus' way of life (**John 14:6**). This is because of the "sin" which lives in us. Instead of doing what is right in God and Jesus' eyes, we would make wrong choices and do what our "flesh" feelings wanted us to do.

Here are some examples: A friend would say or do something to you in passing that offended you. The words, or gesture, more likely, caused you to secretly hold a grudge. You didn't realize it at the time, but you were sinning by holding a grudge. The grudge is the sin of unforgiveness (**Matthew 6:12, 14-15**).

Here is a second example: You would feel as if you didn't have the time to give a friend a call to talk for a while. This would be the sin of being selfish with your time. Your time and agenda would be more important to you than your friend (**Matthew 23:11-12**).

Here is a third example: You would give too much of your time to others when it would be your family who actually needed your help. This is the sin of exalting yourself in front of others so you could receive the credit from them (**Matthew 6:1** & **I Timothy 5:8**).

And here is a fourth example: Let's say you were "on call" for your company. But when a call came in, you resented it, because you were too tired to go out. This is the sin of resentment (**Romans 2:8**). The list could go on and on.

Jesus calls these acts doing the things that our flesh (our personality) wants us to do. And because they are against Jesus' teachings, they were sins we were probably not even aware we were doing.

Eventually we would be introduced to Jesus by a person inviting us to go to church with them. Or, by hearing a Christian program that talked about salvation. This sounded good to us, so we asked Jesus into our hearts! Now that this has happened, we have added a third part to our bodies. We have asked a new Spirit to come in and live on the inside of us. This is the Spirit of God!

"For I delight in the law of God *after the inward man*:"

Romans 7:22

"That which is born of the flesh is flesh; and that which is *born of the Spirit is spirit*."

John 3:6

But when this "New Man" (God's Spirit) came to live on the inside of us, Jesus did NOT remove the spirit of the flesh (the spirit of Satan) from our body. Nor did He automatically change our spirit from being bad and good to being all good. He left this work up to us to do. This is why He told us in **Matthew 12:33** it was up to us to either make our own tree all good or—*it will become all corrupt* (**Haggai 2:11-14**). And this is why Paul tells us in **Romans 7:15-24** and **Galatians 5:17** we have two different sections of our body who fight, one against the other.

Our flesh, which consists of our sin, our soul, our sin feelings, our minds, and our wills (**Hebrews 4:12**) (in other words our personalities), have lived the way that has been RIGHT in their eyes, for years (**Proverbs 16:25** & **John 3:1-6**)!

Now, all of a sudden, a "NEW MAN" is living on the inside of us (**John 3:1-18**). And, He is telling us we must change our thinking into a NEW way of thinking (**Matthew 11:29** & **Ephesians 4:20-25**)! If we choose to change our thinking to the way God and Jesus thinks, then this will cause us to change our soul(s), our sin feelings and our will(s) (**Hebrews 4:12**) (our personalities, personality) from being bad and good (**Genesis 3:5**), to being all good (**Ephesians 4:20-25** & **Romans 12:2**). But, our mind(s) and will(s), *__will fight back against this "NEW way of thinking"__* (**II Corinthians 10:4-6**)!!

What is wrong with this "New God-given Spirit"? I have always been right in the past (**Proverbs 21:2**). And currently I am being told that my choices in life have been all wrong (**Proverbs 3:5-6**)! Who can prove this point out to me?!

No one can! Even God and Jesus Themselves CANNOT make your mind turn around. You must do God and Jesus' way of life, because YOU want to, from the inside out (**Isaiah 55:7-11** & **John 14:6**)!

> "And if it <u>seem evil</u> unto you to serve the LORD, choose you this day whom ye will serve; . . ."

> **Joshua 24:15A**

This is why Jesus did NOT remove our "old man" (our flesh) from us (**Ephesians 4:22**). You are the one who must choose to overcome your flesh (your sin) ON YOUR OWN (**John 8:34-35** & **Romans 6:16**)!!

As for me and my house we agree with Joshua. We choose to serve the LORD. Hell and all the demons that live in hell are NOT the way to go!

> "Then shall he say also unto them on the left hand, Depart from me, ye cursed, into everlasting fire, ***prepared for the devil and his angels***:"
>
> **Matthew 25:41**

If you do NOT believe the Bible, then nothing can be done for you! But if you choose to believe Jesus' Words, then you will need to know: Hell was made for the devil and all of his demons. It was NOT made for people. Hell is a mean and cold place. This means there is NO compassion and NO one cares for you or your feelings!

It is constantly HOT because there is a continuous fire in the center of the earth. This is why we have volcanoes and underground heat. **Isaiah 5:14** tells us *hell enlarges herself without measure to allow the proud and pompous people to enter into it*. When the fire expands, the excess fire has to go somewhere, so it explodes up through the volcanoes.

It has been said, a hole was dug so deep in the earth that the people on top could hear the screams from the people in Hell. The men became so afraid they covered up the hole and abandoned their jobs.

This is one of the rare times I will tell you my personal feelings. There is a lot of love that flows through me to YOU. This is the LOVE of the Father and His Son. Hell is real!! Please do NOT love your "flesh man" so much you will let him deceive you to the point you end your life in HELL!! This is what Jesus means when He tells us in **Revelation 12:11** that "they loved ___not___ their lives unto the death".

It is so much easier to defeat this spirit of good and evil (**Genesis 3:5**), than it is to suffer the rest of your life in hell!!

Compared to how much we would suffer in hell if we end our lives there, defeating our sin (our flesh who lives in us) IS "soo" much easier (**Matthew 11:30**). Jesus tells us in **Mark 9:43-48** that hell's fire is never quenched. And our worm never dies. This means, we will experience this torture forever and ever. Do you really want this for your life?

Let's return to the bitter words. Jesus sends people into our lives to offend this "sin spirit" (this old man; this sin man) which lives on the inside of us. When our "sin man" is offended, he will send all kinds of evil thoughts, resentments, bitter attitudes, and revenges into our mind(s).

Jesus wants this to happen! He wants these thoughts and attitudes to rise from the inside of our soul(s) to the forefront of our mind(s). He doesn't want us to get embarrassed!! This process will happen to us! It was planned! We will see this as we read on. Since the phrase, (THE SIN MAN) was used, we will study this statement from the scriptures in our next lesson.

CHAPTER 18

The Sin Man

WE ARE NOW STARTING to search out the areas in Jesus' Gospel where He is talking to His church heart to heart. He is NOT out to harm the man or woman personally. But, He has to go through the man or woman's mind to get to the human being's flesh.

You see, God cannot bless the sin which lives on the inside of His Christians (**Isaiah 59:1-3**). Therefore, the Holy Spirit is trying to deal with our flesh without crushing God's Spirit that lives on the inside of us. Nor does He want to hurt us as the men and women He created (**Genesis Ch. 2** & **Matthew 19:4-6**).

It is **not** the Holy Spirit's intent to harm our personalities! However, He wants us to recognize the sin that survives within our bodies so we can crucify our sin, not our personalities (**John 15:13** & **Romans 6:6**). Once this flesh is dead and gone, our personality will change from having wrong training to having God and Jesus' training (**Isaiah 55:7-11; Matthew 11:28-30; John 6:14; I Corinthians 2:16** & **Philippians 2:5**).

When this act is completed, God can bless us as being the MEN AND WOMEN we are (**Malachi 3:10; Luke 6:38** & **John 10:10**). Again, you need to know, it is NOT the people themselves God is against, but the "sin" spirit, the flesh, the "old man" who lives within our bodies (**Matthew 5:29-30** & **18:7-9**). It is the part of the human being Adam gave over to Satan (**Genesis 3:6**). It is this part of our bodies who has lived with us since our birth. And he/she has Satan's attitude. This is why he/she is called the old man in **Romans 6:6.**

You see, it is this part of our body which will ruin us, if we let it. Because it is the "old man", the "flesh", the "sin" *__which lives in us__*, who came to steal, kill, and destroy us.

> "The thief cometh not, but for to steal, and to kill, and to destroy: . . ."

John 10:10A

It has been said by the Satanist people, the devil is NOT even worried about the Christian community anymore. All he has to do is to sit back and watch the Christians destroy themselves. He knows it is our own flesh and our own sins which go against Jesus' teachings, who is the thief which is doing the stealing, killing, and destroying (**John 10:10A**).

The Christian community believes Satan is defeated in our lives. And yes, our beautiful Savior did defeat Satan. However, He did NOT defeat the flesh, the sin or the "old man" who lives on the inside of us. This is our choice (**Romans 6:16**). Overcoming our sin, our flesh, our "old man" is the same act as salvation. We must choose to receive Jesus' power to overcome our own flesh, the same way we chose salvation (**Matthew 28:18**).

Jesus died on the cross for the WHOLE world. But, it is ONLY the people who will receive Y'shua as their Savior who receive the benefit of Jesus' wonderful accomplishment (**John Ch. 3**). And overcoming our own sin is the same choice.

You see, when we accepted our Master as our Savior, we received Him on the inside of us. But He did NOT destroy the sin on the inside of us (**Matthew 5:29-30; 7:13-20; 12:33-37; 15:18-20; Ch.18; Mark 7:20-23 & 9:43-48**). This fact is evident if you look at how the Christian community lives in today's world.

Sometimes, we do more things against Jesus' Words than the unbeliever does. For example, we will give a pledge to a ministry because we are moved to do so. But when it comes to fulfilling our pledge, many times our own obligations get in the way; and we cannot follow through. Do you think this act goes unnoticed? Satan and the unbeliever observe us daily (**Hebrews 12:1 & Revelation 12:10B**). Thus, Satan is NOT worried about us, because he knows we will not be faithful to our words!

People—sometimes our prayers go much farther than our money. When your obligations get in your way, don't just lose your commitment. Pray for the ministry instead of just overlooking your pledge. You go to God and tell Him your situation. Tell Him that you would like to complete your pledge to the ministry, but expenses came up you didn't foresee. Therefore, because of life, you cannot finish your pledge at this time. So, would He (God) please move in the heart of the people who could afford it, to please increase their giving (**Proverbs 21:1**)? This would keep the ministry up financially even though you couldn't help at this time.

Satan and his demons will also be required to see your dedication (**Hebrews 12:1**). And then they cannot accuse you before God!

> "And I heard a loud voice saying in heaven, Now is come
> the salvation, and strength, and the kingdom of our God,
> and the power of his Christl: *__for the accuser of our brethren__*

is cast down, which accused them before our God day and
night."

Revelation 12: 10

We don't realize how much we are being watched by Satan and his demons. When he sees us doing the acts against Jesus' teachings, he DOES go to God and he DOES accuse us of doing wrong!!

As long as we allow our flesh to rule our lives, there is not much God or Jesus can do for us. Remember? As long as we are giving into our flesh and letting it rule our lives, we are still sinning (**John 8:34**)! And sin ruins our credit of doing the good in our lives (**Matthew 12:33-34** & **John 15:16**).

> "But we are all as an unclean thing, and all our righteousnesses are as filthy rags; and we all do fade as a leaf; and our iniquities, like the wind, have taken us away."

Isaiah 64:6

Therefore, Jesus cannot cover our sins with His blood until we stop letting our flesh rule our lives (**Matthew 5:19A** & **I John 1:7**).

> "Nay, ye do wrong, and defraud, and that your brethren.
> *Know ye not that the unrighteous shall not inherit the*
> *kingdom of God? . . ."*

I Corinthians 6:8-9A

> "**Mortify therefore your members**, which are upon the earth; fornication, uncleanness, inordinate affection, evil concupiscence, and covetousness, which is idolatry: *For*

*which things sake the wrath of God cometh on the children of
disobedience*:"

Colossians 3:5-6

Remember? The disobedient children are the Christians who disobey
Jesus' Gospel. These are the believers who will read the scriptures.
They will go to church and all the extra church meetings (such as
an extra evangelistic meeting at the church). But, these people are
told, it doesn't matter whether you take heed and DO the teachings
or not; you are still going to heaven at the end of your life (**James
2:14-26**). Also, they are told over and over again, doing God's law is
NOT required by Jesus to be able for Him to justify you (**Romans
2:13** & **Galatians Ch. 3**). Therefore, most Christians DO NOT
complete Jesus' Words! And they become the disobedient Christians
(**II Thessalonians 1:7-9**)!

The unbeliever (the person who claims to be a Christian but is not)
is NOT asked to obey Jesus' Gospel. They cannot be asked to do so
because they do NOT understand Y'shua's teachings. They do NOT
have the Holy Spirit to teach them. They cannot ask Him for His
help unless they accept Jesus first (**I Corinthians 12:3**). Thus, they
are NOT considered to be the disobedient people who do NOT obey
Jesus' Gospel in **Colossians 3:5-6** & **II Thessalonians 1:8-9**.

But we have the Holy Spirit to teach us, thus we CAN be asked,
because of Him!

> "These things have I spoken unto you in proverbs: but
> the time cometh, when I shall no more speak unto you in
> proverbs, but I shall shew you plainly of the Father."

John 16:25

How will Jesus speak to us plainly?

> "Howbeit when he, the Spirit of truth, is come, he will guide you into all truth: for he shall **not** speak of himself; but whatsoever he shall hear, that shall he speak: ___and he will shew you things to come___."

> **John 16:13**

We are the ones who are asked to obey Jesus' Gospel (**Matthew 5:17-19**). And if we choose NOT to do so, then we must pay the price; because, disobeying by not doing Jesus' Words is sin (**I Samuel Ch. 15** & **Luke 15:11-24**). This is how our OWN sin, our OWN flesh, kills, steals and destroys us!!

This is why Jesus and the Holy Spirit are working so hard to help us recognize the "old man" who lives in our body!! This is so, we can destroy him.

> "Knowing this, that our old man is crucified with him, ___that the body of sin might be destroyed___, that henceforth we should ___not___ serve sin. For he that is dead is freed from sin."

> **Romans 6:6-7**

Let's look at Jesus' first step of conquering the "old man" in our next chapter.

CHAPTER 19

Doing Jesus' Words I

D O YOU REMEMBER? IN an earlier chapter, the Holy Spirit
referred to the fact it was actually Jesus who is sending the
sword of the bitter words against us. Since we didn't go into details
on this fact, we will address this truth now.

> **"Think not that I am come to send peace on earth: *I came*
> *NOT to send* peace, but *a sword*."**

> Matthew 10:34

Do you remember the turmoil Sue was feeling after she had been
offended by her friend? When she went to God to look for Him to
defend her, HE told her that she was the one who was sinning just
because she was trying to defend herself and make things right. This
truth caused Sue to become angry at God. She wanted to just back
away and not do Jesus' Words at all. This was **Luke 8:13** taking
place in Sue's life. These bitter words caused *turmoil* in Sue's mind.
And this same kind of turmoil will cause our mind(s) to battle, as well.

Jesus calls the battle which takes place in our mind(s) *the FIRE of
His baptism* in **Luke 12:49-53**. Or it is called the burning of the heart
in **James 3:1-6**. Or it is called being put into the fiery furnace of
affliction in **Isaiah 48:10**. This is why the bitter words are the sword

which causes division. The division causes fire or turmoil in **Luke 12:49-53** & **Matthew 10:34-38**. This same division and battle is the FIRE which will try our work in **I Corinthians 3:10-15**.

The battle comes from the fact our "sin man" has been offended and wants justice. So, he tells our mind(s) we are hurt. And we want our hurt feeling(s) to be able to retaliate and revenge (**Romans 12:16-21**). But Jesus tells us to deny our hurt feelings and just forgive the person who offended us (**Matthew 5:38-39; 16:24** & **Mark 8:34**).

Now our mind(s) has/have a decision to make. Are we going to stay at odds with our accuser and Jesus because of the sword? Are we going to give into our hurt feeling(s) and demand our accuser and God and Jesus to apologize, because of the bitter words? Or, are we going to calm down and listen to Jesus' Words? This is our fire, sword, and battle!

> "And the tongue is a **fire,** . . ."
>
> **James 3:6A**

> "I am come to send **fire** on the earth; . . ."
>
> **Luke 12:49A**

As was just explained to you, Jesus tells us, this fire and sword are His division (His variance) that He **_will_** send against us. In other words, He came to this earth to set our hearts and minds on fire, or in turmoil, and to put us at odds against one another and Himself.

> "_For I am come to set a man at variance_ against his father, and daughter against her mother, and the daughter in law

against her mother in law, And a man's foes shall be they of his own household."

Matthew 10:35-36

"*Suppose ye that I am come to give peace on earth? I tell you, Nay; but rather division*: For from henceforth there shall be five in one house divided, three against two, and two against three."

Luke 12:51-52

Why would Jesus come to this earth to divide us against one another and Himself? Because being offended by our loved ones is the best way to learn how to prevail over our sin.

You see, when the people around us, offend us, it is our own personal spirit of offensiveness which is attacked by the bitter words (**Matthew 18:7-9**). In other words, it is *our sin*, *our flesh of offensiveness*, which is our indignation, revenge, resentment, defensiveness and/or bitterness which will be attacked by the sword. The sword will cause these sin feelings (which live down in the depth of our heart(s)) to rise into our conscious mind(s) (**Matthew 15:16-20** & **Mark 7:18-23**). This is what Jesus wants!

Why?

So we can know beyond a shadow of a doubt our sin still lives on the inside of us (**Romans 7:15-24** & **Galatians 5:15-17**).

Why, you ask?

So we can confess our sins to Jesus. And get rid of them.

"Is any sick among you? let him call for the elders of the church; and let them pray over him, anointing him with oil in the name of the Lord: And the prayer of faith shall save the sick, and the Lord shall raise him up; and if he have committed sins, they shall be forgiven him. Confess your faults one to another, and pray one for another, that ye may be healed. The effectual fervent prayer of a righteous man availeth much."

James 5:14-16

"If we confess our sins, he is faithful and just to forgive us our sins, and to cleanse us from all unrighteousness."

I John 1:9

The ministers teach us, if we confess our sins in the Sinner's Prayer and denounce them all at one time, in general; God will forgive our sins.

Unfortunately, God doesn't agree with this teaching. He will NOT forgive our sins unless we acknowledge them one at a time. Jesus tells us in **John 14:6** it is *HIS way of life only* which allows us to get to the Father. And Jesus teaches us in **Luke 15:11-32** it is only when we acknowledge our own sins one at a time, out loud and before God that He will forgive us.

It has to be YOU personally who has to **face** YOUR own personal sins. It has to be YOU personally who has to **acknowledge** the sins *you have done* in your life. It has to be YOU personally who must **confess** to God and Jesus the sins YOU have committed. And YOU must confess them **one at a time**. This means YOU must speak the sin you have committed out of YOUR mouth and out loud. This is so that YOU and *your cloud of witnesses* can hear YOU speak the sin!!

"WHEREFORE seeing *we also are compassed about with so great a cloud of witnesses*, let us lay aside every weight, *and the sin* which doth so easily beset us, and let us run with patience the race that is set before us,"

Hebrews 12:1

Let's study what Jesus has to say about the prodigal son's sin and what the Holy Spirit teaches about King David's sin with Bath-sheba? Both of these men were in God's Kingdom before they fell into sin (**Luke 15:11-12** & **II Samuel 11:1**). While they were sinning, God was quiet. BUT He remained quiet because both men were guilty of the sins they were committing (**Luke 15:13-16** & **II Samuel Ch. 11**).

Both of these men were unforgiven because they were sinning. Remember, God didn't forgive King David until he came to his senses and asked God to forgive him (**II Samuel 12:13**). And the prodigal son wasn't forgiven until he went to his father, confessed his sin, and asked his father to forgive him (**Luke 15:17-24**). Read the proof of these words.

There is too much scripture to copy in **II Samuel Ch. 11; 12:1-12**, but if you will turn to this scripture and read it with open eyes, you will see God did NOT forgive David of his sin until he confessed it to Him. King David had to; first acknowledge his sin individually (**II Samuel 12:5-12**). And then he had to confess it out loud.

"And David said unto Nathan, I have SINNED against the LORD . . . ."

II Samuel 12:13A

Take note of this fact. It wasn't until after the King had acknowledged this one sin and confessed it out of his mouth, that Nathan was free to tell David he was forgiven. Not all of King David's sins were forgiven all at one time. It was only when he acknowledged one sin at one time; that God could forgive Him (**II Samuel Ch. 24; Psalm 51:2-3 & Psalm 32:5**).

> ". . . And Nathan said unto David, The LORD also hath put away thy sin; thou shalt not die."

> **II Samuel 12:13B**

This man wasn't going to be allowed to live in God's Kingdom after death while he was sinning (**Exodus 32:33 & Ezekiel 18:24**). It wasn't until after the King acknowledged his sin and confessed it out loud to God and before Nathan, that God forgave David and told him, he would not die. Remember, if you go to heaven and live, you have not died because you are living in heaven. But God didn't tell David this act was granted to him until after the King confessed his sin to God and before Nathan (**II Samuel 12:13B**). The same thing was true for the prodigal son. Remember what the father said about his son? *He confessed his son was **dead and lost** while he was sinning.*

> "For this my son was DEAD, . . . *he was LOST*, . . ."

> **Luke 15:24A, C**

It wasn't until after the son came to himself, by acknowledging his sin, and confessing it out loud to God in **Luke 15:17-19,** that he began to come out from under the curse he was in. This acknowledgement and confession was only the beginning of coming out from under. The son had to follow through. He did go to his father. He did confess his sin to his father, and he did ask his father if he could become one of his servants (**Luke 15:20-21**). Once he confessed to his father (the person on this earth who he had sinned against) and asked for his father's forgiveness, *then and only then*, could his father claim his son was now living AGAIN *and* he was now found!

> "And the son said unto him, Father, I have SINNED against heaven, and in thy sight, and am no more worthy to be called thy son."

> **Luke 15:21**

> "For this my son *was dead*, and *is alive AGAIN*; he was lost, and *is found*. And they began to be merry."

> **Luke 15:24**

Get the revelation! The son was alive AGAIN. This means the son was alive BEFORE he fell into sin (**Luke 15:11-12**). But when he sinned, the sin caused the son to become dead (**Ezekiel 18:24; Matthew 13:41 & Luke 13:1-5**). And he stayed dead until he acknowledged the sin he was committing and chose to STOP doing it (**Luke 15:13-19, 24A**).

This is from the New Testament. This is *Jesus' Words written in red*. This is the way the New Testament believers will be judged!! The prodigal son was already in God's Kingdom before he fell into sin. While he was sinning and did NOT acknowledge this fact, the boy (the man) was dead in both his father's and Jesus' eyes (**Luke 15:24**)!!

Do not think—this is just a story about a boy written in the New Testament. We are told, God is NOT a respecter of people. What He does for one person, HE WILL DO FOR THE OTHER (**Romans**

2:11-13). Therefore, if the prodigal son had to acknowledge his sins to receive God's forgiveness we must do it as well!!

> "But he that doeth wrong shall receive for the wrong which
> he hath done: and there is no respect of persons."

Colossians 3:25

We must acknowledge our SINS. We must confess them to God individually and STOP doing them, or we will NOT be forgiven by God!! And if at all possible, we must also apologize *to the person* who we sinned against as well (**Luke 15:18-21**).

Read **Matthew 18:21-35** with an open heart!! Jesus lets us know the person who had been forgiven by God in **Matthew 18:23-27** is now **NOT** forgiven in **Matthew 18:28-35**. Jesus tells us in **Matthew 18:32-34**, God is NOW _wroth_ with the SAME person He had forgiven earlier.

> "And his lord was WROTH, and delivered him to the
> tormentors, till he should pay all that was due unto him."

Matthew 18:34

The forgiveness we thought we received by praying the sinner's prayer is not given to us unless we DO Jesus' Words! And we must DO His Words in the WAY *He tells us to do them*!

> "Jesus saith unto him, _I am the way_, the truth, and the life:
> _no man cometh_ unto the Father, but by me."

John 14:6

Get the revelation people! Jesus' WAY of life is the ONLY way we are going to get to the Father!! And He tells us in **Luke 13:1-5** we MUST REPENT, or WE WILL PERISH!! Remember: what Jesus tells us that applies to the people in the Bible, also applies to us personally. Neither God, nor Jesus will respect one person over another (**Matthew 25:40 & 45**).

Believe me; we do NOT want to perish under God's wrath!! It will be worse for us than it will be for the unbeliever!!

> "For it had been better for them not to have known the way of righteousness, than, after they have known it, to turn from the holy commandment delivered unto them."

II Peter 2:21

Therefore, after we have been offended, let's put down our pride and go humbly to God, acknowledge and confess to Him our SINS individually as they enter into our mind(s)!! This is ONE of the main ways to cast our sin out of our body/bodies!!!

This is important! Many people think they have sinned because they have thoughts of revenge, which will enter into their minds after they have been offended (**James 1:13**). These thoughts are not sin (**James 1:13-14**). Again this is important to know. The thoughts are your temptation to SIN (**James 13:14**). But they are NOT sin until YOU DO what the thoughts are telling you to do (**James 13:15**).

Jesus wants the bad thoughts to surface to our consciousness. However, Paul tells us in **II Corinthians 10:4-5** to cast down our imaginations and bad thoughts. So, when the evil thoughts do surface, most people become embarrassed and they cast them down and out of their minds. Still, because the evil thoughts were NOT confessed to God and Jesus, instead of leaving the Christian's body, these sin feeling(s) will go back down into the Christian's heart again. And then they will resurface in another time and place.

Go ahead and confess them before YOU begin to respect the thoughts and do what they are telling you to do. In other words, respect Jesus' words MORE than you respect your own thoughts/wants (**Matthew 16:24; Mark 8:34 & John 12:48**).

> "Trust in the LORD with all thine heart; and lean not unto thine own understanding. In all thy ways acknowledge him, and he shall direct thy paths."

Proverbs 3:5-6

Remember when the Holy Spirit expressed the fact that, God and Jesus have three ways They were going to use, to get us to recognize our sins? The first was to send a person to us directly to tell us of a sin in which they observed us doing (**Matthew 18:15-17**).

If this direct approach was not received, then the second way is to offend us. After being offended, our flesh will send the bad thoughts and mean words into our minds. When they surface into our minds, God, Jesus and the Holy Spirit are hoping we will acknowledge our sin feeling(s): and handle them (**Matthew 18:7-9**). These are the two main ways Y'shua will cause us to become aware of our sins.

There is one more way I can find in the scriptures. God will allow circumstances to cause us to become aware of our sins. This is what happened to the prodigal son in **Luke 15:13-24**. He ran into the curse of the famine because he did waste his substance and couldn't afford to move to another part of the world (**Luke 15:13-16 & Deuteronomy 28:15-25**). This curse was a direct result from his sin

(**Romans 6:23A**). Eventually, he was wise enough to realize this fact and did repent (**Luke 15:11-24**)!!

But, in today's world, most people don't recognize their circumstances as being a result of their sin. They have been told so many times, "Because we live in a fallen world, bad things just happen to good people", they believe this statement. They believe it so much, they won't acknowledge that their situations could be a result of their sins. So, again, the only way left is for God and Jesus to send us the sword of the bitter words (**Matthew 10:34-38; 18:7** & **Luke 12:49-53**).

Let's read Jesus' next set of instructions in our next chapter.

CHAPTER 20

Disappointment

I N THIS CHAPTER WE will pick up Jesus' Words in **Matthew 13:18-21**. Do you remember in earlier chapters that we were told we must cast the rocks (our sins) out of our body? This is so our promise can grow a deep root down into the ground of our hearts.

Let's return to Jesus' Words.

> *"But he that received the seed into stony places, the same is he that heareth the word, and anon with joy receiveth it;* **Yet hath he not root in himself,** *but dureth for a while: for when tribulation or persecution ariseth because of the word, by and by he is offended."*

Matthew 13:20-21

We are learning how we are to plant our promise into our souls so we can have a deep root in our heart(s). Consequently, God can manifest our promise in our lives. We found out, our heavenly Father cannot help us out of our problems because our sins (our rocks) are in His way (**Isaiah 59:1-3** & **James 4:1-3**). How are our sins in God's way? If you will read on with patience in your heart, the Holy Spirit will explain.

Our Creator only answers prayers through and as according to the written Word of God. In other words, God or Jesus only helps us with our tribulations, afflictions, temptations and/or persecutions if scripture is applied in our lives.

For example, if we ask God to help us financially He will only help us as according to the Bible Words (**Deuteronomy 8:18** & **Proverbs 28:13**). If we ask Him for our health, He will only help us as according to His Bible promise (**Matthew 13:15**). If we ask Him to help us with relationships, it will be as according to the written Word (**John 15:12-13** & **I John 1:7**). This is the way all problems are overcome in life (**Matthew 13:18-23; Mark 4:14-20** & **Luke 8:11-15**). Jesus is the living proof of this fact.

While the Son of God was living on this earth, the written Word was the only way Jesus could overcome His adversities. For example, when Satan tempted our Lord in the wilderness, He had to use the written Word to back Satan off of His life (**Matthew 4:1-11** & **Luke 4:1-13**). Every time Jesus was accused by the scribes, Pharisees or anyone, He answered His accusers with the written Word. **Matthew 9:9-13; 15:1-14; 16:21-28** & **John 7:1-8** are just some examples of this fact. Every time Jesus created a miracle (such as healing the sick, or casting out devils) He used the written Word of God (**Luke 4:14-21**). Nothing but scripture came out of Jesus' mouth, because He knew it took and takes scripture to overcome life (**Psalm 138:2**).

We are NOT above the Holy Son of God (**Matthew 10:24-25; John 13:16-17** & **15:20**). Therefore if Jesus had to use scripture to overcome Satan and all His adversities, then we also must use the written Word to be able to overcome our problems as well (**John 14:12; I Peter 2:21** & **I John 2:6**). This is the only way God or Jesus will be able to help us because it is only the written Word, Satan cannot change (**Genesis 3:1-5**).

We are human, and not above Satan. Nor have we lived as long as he has lived (**Isaiah 14:12-20**). Therefore, he can take our information which isn't written down, and turn it around for his benefit. This is how he deceived Eve (**Genesis 3:1-5**). But, if we quote scripture to Satan, he cannot override the written Word (**Psalm 138:2 & Matthew 4: 1-11**). This is why God sends us to His Word to find His written promises when we ask for His help.

Once we find our promise we are told to meditate so it can be planted down into our heart (**Matthew 13:18-19**). When we do and the plant begins to grow, this is good because God can use this scripture to answer our prayers. The example is in Chapter 6 of this book. The Holy Spirit used God's promise in **Psalm 37:25** to cause the person to receive his/her employment.

But there is still a problem with the employed person as there is with us all. Even though we have learned how to plant our promise into our hearts by meditating, this meditation has not removed the rocks (sins) from our hearts. So our plant has grown a root only until it has hit one of our rocks (sin(s) which live in our heart(s)). When this happens, the root to our promise stops growing. And because the root is still shallow, our promise can wither and die. Thus, the person could end up losing their employment because there is no more promise left to stand on.

Let's look at this from the scriptures. Jesus tells us in **Matthew 13:21** the root to God's promise is shallow because it has only grown until it has hit a rock (sin). In the case of the person who received his/her employment because he/she meditated on **Psalm 37:25**, we are going to say, gossip is one of her/his sins which lives in his/her heart. So, God has allowed the person to be tested for the purpose of learning how to overcome and remove the sin of gossip from his/her body.

Although most people do not understand the purpose of our persecution, this fact does not STOP it from attacking us (**Matthew 5:10 & 10:34**). Thus, it does. Let's take the example of the person in Chapter 6. Because he/she meditated, this person received his/her occupation. He/she has meditated and received the employment. Again, this is **Matthew 13:20; Mark 4:16 & Luke 8:13A** taking place in the person's life. She/he will work at the office in peace for a while. This is the person enduring over a period of time in **Matthew 13:21B; Mark 4:17B & Luke 8:13D**. After some time has passed God will allow the persecution of gossip to attack the person. This is being offended for the Word's sake in **Matthew 13:21C & Mark 4:17C**.

Remember, he/she is the one who has received his/her promise on the rocky ground. Thus, even though the person has meditated, the meditation did NOT remove the rocks (sin(s) from the person's heart). Therefore, the rocky ground means, there are sins in the heart which must be handled by the person. And through the example of the person in Chapter 6, Jesus is going to show you one of His ways of handling the persecution.

Just for clarity, let's call this person Sally. (I chose Sally because I don't know anyone by this name). Nor do I know anyone who has lived through the trial of gossiping. But I do know gossip is a big sin which is liked by office employees. I have never worked in an office under these conditions, so this situation has never happened to me, or anyone I know. It is just not a sin which has plagued our family. But believe me, other sins have. This is just an example to show you how you can overcome sin Jesus' way.

Even though God was able to help Sally obtain her employment, it still takes scripture to keep the rest of the world's problems out of people's lives. For example, the employment was established, but now the curses of life have caused Sally to come across a lady who likes to gossip. And the pressure is on to be a part of the conversation or to be tagged as a trouble maker. What is Sally going to do?? She still needs this job!! Is she going to stay faithful to scripture, or does she take the easy way out?

The temptation is to join in on the fun, be accepted as a part of the team and keep her employment. Or does she remember how she landed the employment and stay faithful to God, and the scriptures, even if it means losing her position? Most people who have been faithful enough to meditate have a root deep enough to want to know how to stay faithful to God and the scriptures and to maintain their employment as well. But, because there isn't any training on how to get this accomplished in life, people fall into giving into the pressure of doing the sin. Let's look at this as an example in Sally's life.

She is the person who received her promise of **Psalm 37:25** with joy in her heart because she landed her job.

> "But he that received the seed into stony places, the same is
> he that heareth the word and anon with joy receiveth it;"

> **Matthew 13:20**

But we must remember this is the person who received her promise on the rocky ground. The meditation caused her to only be able to receive employment; it did NOT remove her rocks (sin(s) which live in her heart). The rocky ground is the person who still has his/her sin(s) in their hearts. And because there are rocks (sin(s) still in the person's heart), the root to her promise has only grown until it has hit the sin of gossip in Sally's heart. Thus, she needs to be tested with the persecution to gossip, to cause this sin to surface into her conscious mind.

You see, Jesus uses the offensiveness of persecution to cause our sins to rise from the inside of our heart(s) to our conscious mind(s). This is why He said in **Matthew 18:7,** offensiveness is needed. This is one of the ways Y'shua purges our bodies of sin (**John 15:2**). This is why He tells us that the trials of persecution come for the word's sake in **Matthew 13:21** & **Mark 4:17.**

In Sally's case, she was born with her parents' sin of gossip way down deep on the inside of her heart. She wasn't even aware she had this sin, until she was confronted with it at the office. This would be **Romans 5:12** taking place in Sally's life. She is finding out, she WANTS to join in on the fun. This would be **James 1:14** taking place in Sally's life. But, she has a big decision she must make.

She has had enough scripture fed to her so she realizes gossip is totally sin (**Exodus 20:16; Psalm 15:3** & **Matthew 5:37; 19:18**). Thus, if she gives into her desire to join in with her co-workers, she realizes she is going against God and His Words.

But, if she stays faithful to God, she is facing the risk of losing her employment. The lady who likes to gossip is the boss' best friend. And has let Sally know, the gossiper will cause her position to be very uncomfortable if she doesn't join in with the team. What is this Christian going to do? She is between a rock and a hard place!

Jesus tells us, if we do NOT know that we are required to go to the scriptures to find another Bible promise to be able to handle this sin, we will become offended and fall into doing the sin. Gossiping will look as if this is the only way Sally will be able to save her job. She could reason out in her mind, "I do need this work to be able to raise my children. And God was good enough to allow me to get it in the first place; so He will forgive my gossiping and allow me to keep it".

This would be **Matthew 13:21; Mark 4:17 & Luke 8:13** taking place in Sally's life.

> "They on the rock are they, which, when they hear, receive the word with joy; and these have no root, which for a while believe, and in time of temptation fall away".

Luke 8:13

Not understanding why the sin of gossiping was presented to her is the (lack of knowledge) in **Isaiah 5:13 & Hosea 4:6**. It was presented to her to let her know this sin was and is rooted down on the inside of her heart. When she realized that she ___did want to join in on the fun,___ this should have been her wake up call (her awareness that the sin was in her heart). Wanting to join in on the fun, but knowing better then to do so, because of scripture, this is being offended for the Word's sake (**Matthew 13:21C & Mark 4:17C**).

It is for the purpose of causing a sin to manifest from the heart into the conscious mind (**James 1:14**). Jesus wants the sin to manifest so the person can confess his/her desire to do the sin (**I John 1:9**).

But again, because Sally didn't know this was the reason this sin was brought to her attention, again because of lack of knowledge, she failed her test and gave into the sin.

When people do not understand what is going on in their lives and they fall into doing the sinning, Jesus considers this act as falling away (**Luke 8:13**). In other words, instead of staying faithful to the scriptures and handling the problem as according to Jesus' Words, Sally gave into doing what was easy to do (**Matthew 16:24-26**). This is falling away from doing what is right in God and Jesus' eyes, and doing what your sin man wants you to do (**Romans 6:16**). This act takes Jesus out of Sally's employment and leaves her open to the world's people to attack her (**Romans 6:23 & James 4:4**).

> "Ye adulterers and adulteresses, know ye not that the friendship of the world is enmity with God? whosoever therefore will be a friend of the world is the enemy of God".

James 4:4

Jesus tells us in **Matthew 13:21; Mark 4:17 & Luke 8:13** because there has not been any meditating on these scriptures, there is NO ROOT on the inside of His Christians. Thus, when we are offended for the Word's sake we will give into the offense and end up sinning. This is **Matthew 13:21; Mark 4:17; Luke 8:13 & James 1:15** taking place in the Christians' lives.

Once we give into the sin, we have allowed a curse to set in on our lives (**James 1:15; Romans 6: 23 & Deuteronomy 28:15-68**). Death, are the curses which come against us. It is the curses of life which kill us, not life itself (**Genesis 3:6-24 & Deuteronomy 28:15-68**). You would find this to be a fact if you read the book of Proverbs with an open heart.

There is way too much scripture to copy to prove this fact to you. However, look what King David had to live under even after he did confess his sin to God (**II Samuel 12:13-II Samuel 24:25**). The rest of his life was always in chaos because he sinned!!

> "For we know him that hath said, Vengeance belongeth unto me, I will recompense, saith the Lord. And again, The

Lord shall judge *his people*. It is a fearful thing to fall into the hands of the living God."

Hebrew 10:30-31

Let's return to Sally's conditions. Even though she has reasoned out in her mind that God will forgive her and let her get away with doing the sin; she still can't get over feeling guilty. She does know better than to out right gossip. When she is alone at night, she cannot shake off the feeling that she has somehow let God down. This is **James 4:4** taking place in Sally's life. She remembers; "It was God who helped me obtain this profession in the first place. And now I am doing something which is hurting His heart. I wish there was some other way than gossiping to be able to retain my position".

> "For the time is come that judgment must begin at the house of God: and if it first begin at us, what shall the end be of them that obey not the gospel of God? And if the righteous scarcely be saved, where shall the ungodly and the sinner appear? Wherefore let them that suffer according to the will of God commit the keeping of their souls to him in well doing, as unto a faithful Creator."

I Peter 4:17-19

Sin, always brings in the curses. However, living your life as according to Jesus' way of life is NOT popular. And many times it leaves you out in the cold, isolated from all other people. This is why Peter tells us in these verses, if you are going to decide to live your life Jesus' way, it is a suffering you may want to consider. Jesus tells us in **Luke 14:26-33** to consider the type of life you will enter into before you enter into it. If you do decide to live as according to Jesus' way of life; you could lose all of your family and friends (**Luke 14:26**). All the people at the office will start to back away from you because you will start to carry God and Jesus' way of life on the inside of you.

> "So likewise, whosoever he be of you that forsaketh ***not all that he hath***, he cannot be my disciple."

Luke 14:33

Your friends at the office, who will begin to back away from you, are a part of the all which you will be forsaking. But, you will be good with God and Jesus. And you will not go to bed with a guilty conscience. Which way is more important to you?

So you can understand what you will be giving up for Jesus' sake, in our next chapter let's study Jesus' way of life.

CHAPTER 21

Victory

L ET'S RETURN TO SALLY'S dilemma at work. Remember? She received her employment because she meditated on God's promise in **Psalm 37:25**. And she worked in her position in peace for a while. This is Sally enduring her promise. This is **Matthew 13:20-21B; Mark 4:16-17B** & **Luke 8:13D** taking place in Sally's life.

> "But he that received the seed into stony places, the same
> is he that heareth the word, and anon with joy receiveth it;
> Yet hath he not root in himself, but dureth for a while:"

Matthew 13:20-21B

Remember, the promise in **Psalm 37:25** was only meditated upon. So it grew down in Sally's heart only until it hit a rock (sin) which was embedded in her heart at birth (**Psalm 58:3; 51:5** & **Romans 5:12**).

She cannot help the fact that this sin was passed on to her at her birth (**Exodus 34:7;** & **John 8:44**). She probably wasn't even aware it existed in her heart. But God and Jesus knew it was there. So, they allowed the temptation to occur in her life. Because the sin is still in her heart, alive and now activated upon **James 1:13-14** has taken place in Sally's heart.

> "Let no man say when he is tempted, I am tempted of God: for God cannot be tempted with evil, neither tempteth he any man: But every man is tempted, when he is drawn away of his own lust, and enticed."

> **James 1:13-14**

The Christian cannot even help the fact that he/she is tempted to join in on the fun and wants to be accepted as a part of the office crowd. This is what sin does to the person. Sally is enticed because of the sin which was embedded in her heart (**James 1:14**).

BUT, what the person *decides* that he/she is going to do with his/her tribulation, or persecution is up to them.

> "Know ye not, that to whom ye yield yourselves servants to obey, his servants ye are to whom ye obey; whether of sin unto death, or of obedience unto righteousness?"

> **Romans 6:16**

The tribulation or persecution in **Matthew 13:21** is the temptation to gossip. This temptation was put in Sally's life to allow the deep rooted sin of gossiping to surface into her conscious mind. This is allowing the tribulation of persecution of being tempted to gossip to enter into the person's life for the Word's sake.

> "Yet hath he not root in himself, but dureth for a while: for __when tribulation or persecution, ariseth because of the word__, . . ."

> **Matthew 13:21A-B**

God and Jesus want this temptation to surface into the Christian's mind. They want the person to be aware that they are tempted to gossip. Why?

So, the person can confess this temptation to himself/herself! In other words, so this person can acknowledge his/her sin which lives within his/her heart.

> "*I acknowledge my sin* unto thee, and mine iniquity have I not hid. I said, I will confess my transgressions unto the Lord; and thou forgavest the iniquity of my sin."
>
> **Psalm 32:5**

> "*And when he came to himself, he said*, How many hired servants of my father's have bread enough and to spare, and I perish with hunger! *I will arise and go to my father, and will say unto him, Father, I have sinned against heaven, and before thee,*"
>
> **Luke 15:17-18**

So far, the person who is tempted to gossip has NOT sinned (**James 1:14**). It is only when the person gives into the temptation and does gossip with the gang that lust has conceived, and the person has sinned.

> "Then when lust hath conceived, it bringeth forth sin: . . ."
>
> **James 1:15A**

Acknowledging the fact (that you WANT to gossip with the gang) is NOT sin. When you finally acknowledge to yourself, this gossip thing at work is working hard on your conscience and you really do want to join in with your co-workers, and you confess this feeling to God and Jesus, this confessing takes away the desire to do this sin.

> "There hath no temptation taken you but such as is common to man: but God is faithful, who will not suffer you to be tempted above that ye are able; but will with the temptation also make a way to escape, that ye may be able to bear it."

I Corinthians 10:13

Now, you no longer have the desire to give into the gossip, you now have another dilemma you are facing. The gossiper is best friends with your boss and she/he has threatened your employment if you stand against her/him. Now what are you going to do? Look at God's promise for this kind of situation.

> "But now thus saith the Lord that created thee, O Jacob, and he that formed thee, O Israel, Fear not: for I have redeemed thee, I have called thee by thy name; thou art mine. When thou passest through the waters, I will be with thee; and through the rivers, they shall not overflow thee: when thou walkest through the fire, thou shalt not be burned; neither shall the flame kindle upon thee. For I am the Lord thy God, the Holy One of Israel, thy Saviour: I gave Egypt for thy ransom, Ethiopia and Seba for thee. Since thou wast precious in my sight, thou hast been honourable, and I have loved thee: therefore will I give men for thee, and people for thy life."

Isaiah 43:1-4

This is a time when I will get personal. I understand your fear, because God has put me in these kinds of positions many times. You are against a rock and a hard place. If you gossip you go against scripture. But if you don't gossip, you could lose your job.

When I was put in this kind of situation, I would tell the person who was persecuting me, "You know, you are strong. And you may have more authority than me, BUT my GOD is stronger than you!! And He HAS more authority than you. Therefore, His promise in **Isaiah 43:1-4** has more value than does your threats."

"Because I needed this job, God is the one who gave it to me. Thus, HE is the **_only One_** who can take it away. Therefore, you cannot have me fired unless my God tells you, you can! And I know that He will not do that because He is the One who landed me this job in the first place."

Don't get me wrong, I never went to the person personally. I said this to God's Holy Spirit in the privacy of my own bedroom. And then I let the Holy Spirit deal with the problem that was facing me (**Ephesians 6:12-18**). I went about my business as if nothing was going on. And when the situation would attack me again, I would again tell the person under my breath, "God is bigger than you." You just keep reminding yourself of **Isaiah 43:1-4** and eventually the gossiping will just cease.

> "When a man's ways please the Lord, he maketh even his enemies to be at peace with him."

> **Proverbs 16:7**

What has just happened? By doing what the scriptures have said, and confessing your desire to give into the sin of gossip, to yourself,

God and Jesus, you have crucified and buried the temptation to do the sin (**Romans 6:1-4).** You have conformed yourself to do as Jesus would have done, had He been in your place (**Romans 6:5**). You have crucified and destroyed the sin of gossip (not only in yourself): but in the office as well (**Romans 6:6**).

But, you need to know. This is when all the office people will start to back away from you. This would be **Romans 8:17** taking place in your life. **Romans 8:17** will begin to take place in your life because you now will be abiding in Jesus' Words and carrying His Life on the inside of your body (**John 15:1-5**). Remember? He lost all His followers except His disciples in **John 6:40-69**.

Although you will become distant from the people in the office, you will become a friend to Jesus.

> "Ye are my friends, if ye do whatsoever I command you."

John 15:14

This is what Peter means when he tells us in **I Peter 2:7-12** that Jesus will become a stumbling stone to the world's people and to the people who do NOT want to live their lives in Jesus' way of life (**John 14:6**). Your life will begin to become offensive to these people (**I Peter 2:7-8**). But to the people who want to live for God and who have Jesus' desires as their desires, this kind of living is music to their ears (**John 15:19-20**). This is why Jesus tells us to study out what His way of living will cost us, and see if it is worth it to you (**Luke 14:26-35**).

Once Sally has won her victory over the gossip, I don't think she wants to live through it again, so she will never be tempted with gossip again (**Romans 6:7**).

> "Knowing this, that our old man is crucified with him, that the body of sin might be destroyed, that henceforth we should not serve sin. For he that is dead is freed from sin."

Romans 6:6-7

Because you have removed the temptation to gossip, now your promise of retaining your employment has grown deeper into your soul, and you are more confident than ever, you will keep your occupation.

> "But that on the good ground are they, which in an honest and good heart, having heard the word, keep it, and bring forth fruit with patience."

Luke 8:15

And because you handled the situation in the same way as Jesus would have handled it, you do not have any curses which will attack your household (**Proverbs 26:2 & 10:22**).

But, if people do NOT understand God and Jesus' ways of life, when the temptation to unite with the co-workers arises, most people will give into the temptation because they don't see any other way to save their jobs. This is the person who has the rocky ground in their heart(s). And because the root of their Bible promise has hit the hardship of a temptation to sin, most people give into the temptation and do the sin. This is why Jesus tells us in **Matthew 13:21; Mark 4:17** and **Luke 8:13** the root of their promise is shallow and when the trial, or tribulation, or affliction comes their way, they give into the trial. This causes them to end up serving their master of sin.

Once they give into this master, then they cannot stop serving it. This is why Paul tells us in **Romans 6:16**, we can make the choice of who we want to serve. We can choose to do what the scriptures are telling us to do and serve obedience unto righteousness. Or we can choose to serve our sin, and then we will end up serving it until we die (**John 8:34-35**).

> "Know ye not, that to whom ye yield yourselves servants to obey, his servants ye are to whom ye obey; whether of sin unto death, or of obedience unto righteousness?"

Romans 6:16

> "Then said Jesus again unto them, I go my way, and ye shall seek me, and shall die in your sins: whither I go, ye cannot come."

John 8:21

This is why it is important for us to be able to understand Jesus' ways of life. Again, it is the only way in which we will be able to make heaven.

> "Jesus saith unto him, I am the way, the truth, and the life: no man cometh unto the Father, but by me."

John 14:6

With this understanding in mind, let's learn another way in which Jesus teaches how we can overcome our sin in the next chapter.

CHAPTER 22

Dealing With Sin

DEALING WITH OUR SINS is hard on our desires. As was shown in our last chapter, we want to be accepted by people. We were born with this desire. Jesus was also. This is why Jesus' brothers hurt His feelings when they let Him know they didn't believe in Him. They told Jesus, "Even You desire to be known by people".

> "Now the Jews' feast of tabernacles was at hand. His brethren therefore said unto him, Depart hence and go into Judaea, that thy disciples also may see the works that thou doest. For there is no man that doeth any thing in secret, ___and he himself seeketh to be known openly___. If thou do these things, shew thyself to the world. ___For neither did his brethren believe in him.___"

> **John 7:2-5**

Jesus did want to be accepted, but not in the way His brothers were saying. Because of His ministry, our Lord was well known. But He was only known because of the miracles He did for the people. It was not because the people really liked Jesus as a friend. It really did hurt our Savior to be rejected. This is why He asked His disciples if they were going to leave Him also, when everyone He talked to in Capernaum walked away from Him (**John 6:24-67**).

"From that time many of his disciples went back, and walked no more with him. Then said Jesus unto the twelve, Will ye also go away?"

John 6:66-67

Jesus wasn't seeking fame and fortune. He just wanted to be accepted as being the person (GOD) He was. He had told His people, He was the living bread which came down from heaven.

"***I am the living bread which came down from heaven***: if any man eat of this bread, he shall live for ever: and the bread that I will give is my flesh, which I will give for the life of the world."

John 6:51

When He wasn't accepted, it DID hurt!! This is how He understands when we are rejected just because we want to live life in His way of life. Like Jesus, it seems as if we stand off by ourselves. And this hurts!! This is the kind of suffering Paul is referring to when he tells us in **Romans 8:17**, we will suffer in the same kind of way Jesus suffered!

"And if children, then heirs; heirs of God, and joint-heirs with Christ; ***if so be that we suffer with him***, that we may be also glorified together."

Romans 8:17

Living through the first trial is always the hardest. If you don't understand what is coming, it could cause you to become offended at Jesus' way of life. And because your family and friends would mean more to you than Jesus' way of life, you could choose to return to your old way of living. This would be sad if you did. Because Jesus tells us in **Matthew 10:34-38**; if you choose your life with your family and friends over, and above, Him; you will lose Him.

> "He that loveth father or mother more than me is not worthy of me: and he that loveth son or daughter more than me is not worthy of me. And he that taketh **not** his cross, and followeth after me, is not worthy of me."

> **Matthew 10:37-38**

Now again you have a choice you must make. Are you going to stay faithful to Jesus' way of life? Or are you going to live with the guilty conscience and live the life which is easy to live and be accepted by family and friends? You need to know, if you fight to keep your acceptance and your social life up with the ones who were rejecting you, and you actually win your battle, you will lose your life with Jesus. But if you lose this kind of life for Jesus' sake, you shall find your eternal life with Him.

> "He that findeth his life shall lose it: and he that loseth his life for my sake shall find it."

> **Matthew 10:39**

> "He that loveth his life shall lose it; and he that hateth his life in this world shall keep it unto life eternal."

> **John 12:25**

In other words, if you choose to live the life where you are accepted by your family and/or friends, and you choose to do the things which cause you to be accepted, you are loving your life in this world. Jesus tells us, "He that loveth his life SHALL LOSE IT;"

In other words, you will not only lose your eternal life with Jesus, but this world's life will not last forever, and you will lose it as well. Once you die, this life is over. And if you choose this life, your life with Jesus will be over as well.

> "For whosoever will save his life shall lose it: and whosoever will lose his life for my sake shall find it."
>
> **Matthew 16:25**

> "And they overcame him by the blood of the Lamb, and by the word of their testimony; ***and they loved not their lives unto the death***."
>
> **Revelation 12:11**

This is hard, Jesus does know. He lived under the SAME pressure you are feeling as you are reading this chapter. He had and has the SAME desires as you. He is hoping you will choose HIM. He desires to live with you. And He is hoping you will desire the same. This is why He even chose to come to this earth and live under all the heartache the world could throw at Him (**Isaiah Ch. 53** & **John Ch. 1 & 3**).

But again, this choice is yours!

If you do choose to go on with Jesus, you can read on. Or you can stop, because He has more suffering coming your way.

One of the "fruits of the Spirit" is longsuffering. The type of suffering as was described for Sally is again the kind of longsuffering which is the "fruits of the Spirit." Jesus tells us up front, "You will face this kind of suffering." He tells you ahead of time so, when it does happen, you will understand and have peace in your heart.

> "These things I have spoken unto you, that in me ye might have peace. In the world ye shall have tribulation: but be of good cheer; I have overcome the world."

> **John 16:33**

> "Remember the word that I said unto you, The servant is NOT greater than his lord, If they have persecuted me, they WILL also persecute YOU; if they have kept my saying, they will keep yours also."

> **John 15:20**

Remember, your tribulation is your persecution (**Matthew 13:21; Mark 4:17** & **Luke 8:13**). And the situation with Sally is just one example of this type of persecution, tribulation, affliction and temptation.

We carry more than one sin in our souls. Therefore, the tribulation given to Sally was just one type of persecution which Jesus will send our way.

> "Think not that I am come to send peace on earth: I came not to send peace, ***but a sword.***"

> **Matthew 10:34**

Remember, the bitter words are the sword Jesus came to this earth to send against us.

> "The ***words of his mouth*** were smoother than butter, but war was in his heart: ***his words*** were softer than oil, yet ***were*** they ***drawn swords***."
>
> **Psalm 55:21**

The sword (bitter words) is sent against us to cause our hearts to be set on fire or in turmoil.

> "And the tongue is a fire, a world of iniquity: . . ."
>
> **James 3:6A-B**

> "I am come to send fire on the earth; . . ."
>
> **Luke 12:49A**

Why? So you will become offended.

> "Woe unto the world because of offences! for it must needs be that offenses come; . . ."
>
> **Matthew 18:7A-B**

Why does this have to happen? So the rest of your hidden sins can surface into your conscience mind!

> "Every branch in me that beareth not fruit he taketh away: and every branch that beareth fruit, ***he purgeth it, that it may bring forth more fruit.***"

John 15:2

Offensiveness causes your sin feelings to rise to the surface of your mind(s). The purging is the purging of your sins from your body. When you recognize that your feelings of defense are your sin feelings and you confess them to God and Jesus, this act clears the feelings from your body (**I John 1:9**). But we still have the root of sin from which the sin feelings are flowing. And this root must be cleared from our bodies, or our sin will continue to send these feelings into our mind(s).

Let's take a look at how our sin can ruin our lives in our next chapter.

CHAPTER 23

Doing Jesus' Words II

YOU NEED TO KNOW this detail up front: there will be facts and scriptures repeated in these lessons. This is because these truths are new to some of you. And it is a proven fact it takes repetition to burn new realities into our consciousness. This is one of the ways in which God teaches us to meditate (**Joshua 1:8**). Doesn't the Holy Spirit tell us in **Joshua 1:8** to study on the scriptures day and night? This cannot be done without repetition! Let's begin.

In Chapter 19, we were studying Jesus' Words in **Luke 15:11-24.** He revealed to us in this lesson, our first step of cutting our flesh out of our body is to confess our own personal sins to Him. This is not as hard to do as one would think. All we have to do is realize how this "old man" is destroying us as human beings and then, we will WANT to get rid of him from the inside out (**Matthew 5:29-30; 18:8-9 &** **Mark 9:43-48**).

This "sin man" wants to survive! He does not want us to identify him. Therefore, he hides in the middle of our heart(s) (souls). He is a master at getting us to submit to his way(s) of life (**Proverbs 12:15; 14:12; 16:2, 25; 21:2 & 24:12**). He will rise up on the inside of our mind(s) and tell us, he is the best friend we have and we cannot get along in this world without him (**Proverbs 12:15; 16:2; 21:2 & 24:12**). He will also tell us he knows what is best for us, and _we would_ *do well to listen to him,* or we will end up in trouble (**Proverbs 12:15; 14:12;** & **16:25**). He is the one who wants to ruin our lives.

Didn't Paul tell us in **Romans 7:15-24** that he wanted to do what he knew was right with God, but he didn't do it? And he didn't want to do what he knew was against God. But this is what he did, even though he knew better.

> "For that which I do I allow not: for what I would, that do I not; but what I hate, that do I. If then I do that which I would not, I consent unto the law that it is good. Now then it is no more I that do it, but sin that dwelleth in me. For I know that in me (that is, in my flesh,) dwelleth no good thing: for to will is present with me; but how to perform that which is good I find not."

> **Romans 7:15-18**

The sin which rides on the inside of us wants us to believe we are the ones who are in charge of our lives, but it is really the "sin man" who wants to control us. You see, if we can discover "him" as the one who wants to manage our lives, instead of it being us (our own qualities) it is much easier to get mad at the one who is ruining our lives.

Let the Holy Spirit show this fact to you from the scriptures.

Jesus tells us in **Matthew 5:28-30; 18:7-9** and **Mark 9:43-48** we are to cut this man off by denying him (**Matthew 16:24** & **Mark 8:34**). And then we are to cast this offending spirit out of our body.

> "Ye have heard that it was said by them of old time, Thou shalt **not** commit adultery: But I say unto you, That whosoever looketh on a woman to lust after her hath

committed adultery with her already in his heart. And if thy right eye offend thee, pluck it out, and cast it from thee: for it is profitable for thee that one of thy members should perish, and not that thy whole body should be cast into hell. And if thy right hand offend thee, cut it off, and cast it from thee: for it is profitable for thee that one of thy members should perish, and not that thy whole body should be cast into hell."

Matthew 5:27-30

Let's think about what was said. Who on the inside of you would *WANT* to outright sin against God, Jesus, the Holy Spirit and/or the people in your life? Would it be you, or the "sin man" who lives on the inside of you?

Do you really have the desire to sin? If you have any conscience at all, once you give into doing a sin which you know is directly against scripture, you do feel guilty. More times than not, you *cannot* shake the feeling that you are hurting the people you love. If you are a Christian, this desire to do the sin is **not** you (your personality). Let's explain this fact.

Once the Christian has accepted Jesus into his/her life; **II Corinthians 5:17-18** tells us we become NEW creatures. This means, we have a New Spirit which is a part of God's Holy Spirit (**John Ch. 3**). This New Spirit will begin to teach our soul(s) about Jesus.

Remember? Our soul(s) is our heart(s) because it is in the center of our personality. Our soul (our flesh) is made up of our mind(s), our feeling(s) and our will(s) (**I Thessalonians 5:23** & **Hebrews 4:12**).

As we learn Jesus' new way(s) of life, our personality will begin to change (**II Corinthians 3:18**). Now we have what Paul calls the carnal mind and the mind of the Spirit (**Romans 8:6**). This is the same double minded man whom James refers to in **James 1:8**. And this is the same double minded man whom Jesus refers to in **Matthew 12:33-34**.

The carnal mind is the part of the mind which has NOT changed (**Romans 8:7; I Corinthians 3:1-3** & **Hebrews 5:9 to 6:6**). It is the carnal part of the mind that would want to sin (**Romans Ch. 7 & 8**). This is why Paul tells us about his fight with his own body in **Romans 7:15-24**. And explains to us in **Galatians 5:17** how the Spirit and flesh will fight against each other.

Jesus tells us in **Matthew 10:1; 28:18; Luke 10:19** and **John 17:1-2** that He gives you (your personality) the power to overcome the serpents, scorpions, and over all the powers of the enemy. This power includes the part of your soul which has NOT changed ("YOUR flesh") (**Matthew 28:18** & **John 17:1-2**).

In other words, Jesus will give your mind, and your will the power to overcome your emotions; but you *MUST want to accept it from the bottom of your will*. You MUST make the choice, it is ***NOT my will*** Father, but I want to fulfil YOUR WILL in my life (**Matthew 6:10; 7:21; John 6:40, 53-54, 56: I John 3:24; Matthew 26:37-45; Mark 14:34-41; Luke 22:39-46;** & **Romans 6:16**).

If you *DO — and you don't* want Jesus' power, then it WILL BE the sin man who WILL WIN (**I Corinthians 3:1-3**). And he WILL SIN for and through you (**John 8:34**). The sad thing is, once you do allow him to sin, on your behalf; you are doomed to obey him (**John 8:34**).

When you do obey your sin by doing his desires (**James 1:14-15**); you open the door to the curses. Let's face the facts. The curses are in the world. What people accept as just being a part of life are really curses.

For example sinus conditions are one of the curses. Some sicknesses are a part of the curses (**Matthew 9:1-7**). And some sicknesses are for the glory of God (**John 9:1-7**). Being poor is a curse. Our farms failing are curses. Destroying weather comes from curses. And I could go on and on. But I don't want to. Go to **Deuteronomy 28:15-68** and study out what the curses are and where they come from. These Words did NOT leave the world just because Jesus was born (**Matthew 5:17-18**). Therefore, they are in this world and they are a part of today's life.

If Paul said in **Galatians 3:13**, Jesus came to redeem us from these curses, then why are we, as His people, suffering under the conditions (curses)? There has to be a reason. Why are the curses being allowed to attack the Christian?

No one wants to own up to the fact; it is your own "sin man" who is ruling your life (**John 10:10**). By listening to this "man", obeying him and doing as he wants you to do you are choosing to obey your sin master instead of doing Jesus' Words.

When we choose to obey our sin, instead of Jesus' Words, this action calls for failure in our lives (**Matthew 7:26-27** & **Luke 6:49**). Jesus doesn't promise us success, He promises us failure. This failure opens the door and allows the curses to attack us (**Matthew 15:16-20; 12:33-37** & **Mark 7:20-23**).

It is your own "sin man" who lives on the inside of your body who wants to kill, steal and destroy your life. He doesn't care if you end your life in hell with him (**Matthew 10:28** & **Luke 12:4-5**). This is his desire (**John 10:10**). He is the one who causes sin to look good.

> "But every man is tempted, when he is *drawn away of his own lust*, and enticed."

> **James 1:14**

But, once we give into obeying his desires, his enticement, his lust, we are doomed because we sinned.

> "Then when lust hath conceived, it bringeth forth sin: and sin, when it is finished, bringeth forth death."

> **James 1:15**

James didn't promise us life. He didn't tell us, even though you sinned, don't worry; Jesus' blood will cover your sin. He told us, this sin will bring death to you. James is talking to the born again believer, not the sinners. This is why he gives us this warning in his next sentence.

> "Do not err, my beloved brethren."

> **James 1:16**

Be careful who you believe. Jesus doesn't promise us success in **Matthew 7:26-27** & **Luke 6:49**. He doesn't tell us, "Don't worry, even though you didn't do My Words in My way of life (**John 14:6**), it will be okay". He said quite to the contrary.

"If a man abide NOT in me, he is cast forth as a branch, and is withered; and men gather them, and cast them into the fire, and they are burned."

John 15:6

Remember the example of Sally. She abided in Jesus, by obeying His Words in **Matthew 19:18**, and standing on God's promise in **Isaiah 43:1-4**. Remember, the gossip stopped, but all of her friends began to back away from her (**Matthew 5:10-11**).

This is because she started to carry Jesus' way of life on the inside of her life. This IS abiding in Jesus and He abiding on the inside of us!! If we don't do this, Jesus doesn't promise us to be able to live with Him. We just read where He tells us, we will be thrown into the fire to burn (**John 15:6**).

But this means, we must decide to become angry with the "the body of sin", the "old man" the "sin", the part of our mind who remained carnal. And we must decide to overcome that part of our minds (**Romans 6:6; 7:20 & 8:6**). He is the one who entices us to give into his desires (**James 1:13-14**). He joins forces with the other people who want to live life so it is good for them (**Proverbs 14:12; 16:2 & Matthew 16:24-26**).

Gossiping is fun and easy to do for a while (**Matthew 16:25-26 & Hebrews 11:25**). And it gives into our sin man's desire to join in on the fun and be accepted (**James 1:13-15A**).

On the surface, it doesn't look as if giving into our sin man's desire to go ahead and sin is going to hurt anyone, or anything. This is the way it is with complaining. It is the same with being grumpy. It is the same with holding grudges. It is the same with revenging. It is the same with being jealous. It is the same with resenting. It is the same with back biting. It is the same with your anger and strife. (This anger is because you didn't get your way; not because you are angry at the sin going on around you).

Jesus' kind of anger is the only kind of anger which isn't sin (**Mark 3:5**). All of these sins look innocent when we are doing them. But, every one of them opens up the door and allows the curses of life to enter into our lives.

> "And he said, That which cometh out of the man, that defileth the man. For from within, out of the heart of men, proceed evil thoughts, adulteries, fornications, murders, Thefts, covetousness, wickedness, deceit, lasciviousness, an evil eye, blasphemy, pride, foolishness: All these evil things come from within, and defile the man."
>
> **Mark 7:20-23**

Once we are defiled, the curses have the right to enter into our lives, and destroy us until we die (**Ezekiel 18:23-24** & **Matthew 12:37B**). Adam and Eve are pure examples of this fact.

Doesn't Paul warn us in **I Corinthians 11:23-30**; be careful how we take our communion with Christ? Because, if we do it wrongly, we do end up suffering under the curses!! Some of the people had so many curses on top of them, that the curses finally brought death (**I Corinthians 11:27-30**). This is **Ezekiel 18:23-24** & **Matthew 12:33-37; 15:18-20** & **Mark 7:20-23** taking place in these people's lives.

Are you beginning to understand how it is your own "sin man" who is the one who is out to destroy you? Wouldn't it be better to identify him for who he is and for us to do Jesus' Words in **Matthew 5:29-30** & **18:7-9** and cast him out of our bodies? Jesus tells us, it is better for us to destroy him, instead of allowing him to destroy us!!

Read Jesus' Words in **Mark 9:42-48**. If we give into this man's desires and allow him to offend our God-given Spirit, we can end our lives in hell. Once we are there, we will never die. The suffering of hell and its fire continues forever. Think about this fact for a few minutes.

Imagine yourself in this fire. See, your flesh burning off your bones. Jesus tells us in **Mark 9:42-48** our worm never dies. This means, you will experience this same punishment over and over again. Therefore, your skin will burn off of your bones over and over again. And **_you will be able to feel the occurrence_** over and over again. See yourself yearning for some water to cool down your body (**Mark 9:42-48** & **Luke 16:20-31**). Is your sin man worth this much to your personality?

> "For what is a man profited, if he shall gain the whole world, and lose his own soul? or what shall a man give in exchange for his soul?"
>
> **Matthew 16:26**

In our next chapter let's study Jesus' Words in **Matthew 5:29-30; 18:7-9** & **Mark 9:42-48**.

CHAPTER 24

Doing Jesus' Words III

IN OUR LAST CHAPTER we were studying how our "sin man" ruins our lives. Therefore Jesus tells us to cut him off and cast him from us so he becomes maimed. Once he is halt, he doesn't have any more power over our bodies (**John 17:1-3** & **Romans 6:7**).

The example of Sally is one way in which Jesus teaches us to cut off our sin (**Romans 6:1-7**). The second way is in **Matthew 10:34-38; 16:24; 18:7-9; Luke 12:41-59;** & **14:26**. This is just a few places were Jesus teaches this lesson.

Let's again return to our original promise. We believe **Malachi 3:10.** We have tithed and meditated. Our promise hits another sin we didn't know we have. Remember, Jesus tells us in **John 15:1-3**, He will purge our bodies of its sin until "***He knows***" we are clean.

After we are clean, Jesus can manifest our promise in our lives (**Proverbs 28:13**). But it will take some time for Him to clear our bodies of our sin. Don't be discouraged. It took a lifetime for us to develop our sins; it will take some time to clear them out of our bodies.

Let's say you are talking to some friends at church. You are sharing some of your beliefs. You are not aware they do not believe the way you do. Your minister is good, so you just assumed everyone believed as was being taught. But there is this one gentleman who attacked your conversation. He lived through many of the curses, so he was bitter. He was promised a better life with Jesus, and when it didn't happen, he became sour and disappointed. So, he was out to prove the scriptures wrong.

Your natural reaction was to defend the scriptures and yourself. But what does Jesus tell us we must do with our defensive system which lives on the inside of us?

> "And when he had called the people unto him with his disciples also, he said unto them, Whosoever will come after me, let him deny himself, and take up his cross, and follow me."

Mark 8:34

We are to allow the gentleman to have his own ideas; do NOT answer him, and just walk away. In other words, do NOT answer any person who offends you in any way. Do NOT argue back with your accusers. And do NOT defend yourself for now. Let the Holy Spirit defend you. Over a period of time, this will prove true.

Jesus knows just how hard this is to do. This is why He wants you to confess these feelings to Him and not to the people who will argue with you. After you get home, tell God and Jesus everything you were feeling at the time you were offended. This confession will clear the feelings from your body.

While you are confessing, ask God to have the Holy Spirit reveal to you what kind of sin your promise hit. Remember, this situation was allowed to cause a sin to surface from the depths of your soul into your conscious mind.

Confess the sin to God, but then cast it out of your body as according to Jesus' instructions in Matthew & Mark. This is how you will cut off your "sin man's" eye, hand and foot. As you cast this sin from your body, you are casting away one of the sins your sin man likes to do. This act maims and halts the man because he now has one less sin he can do.

> "Wherefore if thy hand or thy foot offend thee, cut them off, and cast them from thee: it is better for thee to enter into life halt, or maimed, rather than have two hands, or two feet to be cast into everlasting fire."

> **Matthew 18:8**

Even though this "old man" would make you think he is your best friend (**Mark 11:21-24**), Jesus tells us to cut "him" (this "sin man") off and cast "him" from us (**Matthew 5:29-30; 18:7-9 & Mark 9:43-48**). Remember: your sin doesn't mind offending, complaining, or becoming grumpy for you. In other words, he doesn't mind sinning on your behalf (**Matthew 15:17-20; 18:7 & Mark 7:20-23**). He doesn't mind causing the men to get hooked on pornographic material. He doesn't mind offending the God-given Spirit who lives on the inside of these men and women.

> "But I say unto you, That whosoever looketh on a woman to lust after her hath committed adultery with her already in his heart. And if thy right eye offend thee, pluck it out, and cast it from thee: for it is profitable for thee that one of thy members would perish, and not that thy whole body

should be cast into hell. And if thy right hand offend thee, cut it off, and cast it from thee: for it is profitable for thee that one of thy members should perish, and not that thy whole body should be cast into hell."

Matthew 5:28-30

In other words, the next time you are enticed by your sin man (**James 1:14**); stop in your tracks and deny it by telling it "No"!!! Confess your feelings to God and Jesus.

Confess that it is really enticing you to give into your sin man's desires at this minute and ask Jesus for the strength to overcome your sin. He will give it to you (**John 17:1-3**). Once you get control over "HIM"; cast the sin of studying pornographic material out of your life. Or cast the sin of holding grudges out of your life. Or cast the sin of strife out of your life. Or cast any other sin which wants control of you, out of your life.

Our "sin man" will try to rise up in the middle of our mind(s) and tell us this instruction is crazy.

Who in his/her right mind would want to pluck out his/her own eye or cut off his/her hand or foot? No one wants to do that.

We all know Jesus' words are NOT crazy! So what is Jesus telling us to do in these scriptures?

He is telling us to cut off the desire to sin, by **not** allowing our "sin man" to rule our lives. He is telling us to make the decision to tell our carnal mind(s) and our offensive feelings they cannot rule over our bodies. He is also telling us to tell our hurt feelings, they CANNOT control our lives (**I Samuel 30:6; Psalm 42:5, 11; 43:5; 56:3-4 Mark 11:23-24**).

Did you know; people believe their OWN words **more** than they believe anyone else's? Therefore; when we purposely choose to talk to our OWN hurt feelings, they must listen to *our choices* in our lives. This is one of the ways we will turn our way of thinking around (**Proverbs 18:21**).

> "But I say unto you, That every idle word that men shall speak, they shall give account thereof in the day of judgment. For by thy words thou shalt be justified, and by thy words thou shalt be condemned."

Matthew 12:36-37

The proof that this fact is true is this: When you decided to become a Christian, there were *no demons in hell who could stop you from doing this deed*! And when you decided to become a Christian, YOUR "sin man" could NOT stop you from accepting Jesus into your life no matter how hard he tried to do so! Therefore, when YOU decide to DO Jesus' Words and be stronger than your sin, there is NOTHING that your sin can do to stop you! Again, the choice is YOURS!!!

> "What man is he that feareth the LORD? him shall he teach in the way that *he shall choose.*"

Psalm 25:12

But you need to know this: When you *do* decide to cut this man off, he WILL try to cause your heart to hurt! This is why Paul tells us the cutting off of our "sin man" is the same thing as cutting into our hearts.

"But he is a Jew, which is one inwardly; and circumcision is that of the **heart**, . . ."

Romans 2:29A

"Circumcise therefore the foreskin of your **heart**, and be no more stiffnecked."

Deuteronomy 10:16

"For we are the circumcision, which worship God in the spirit, and rejoice in Christ Jesus, and have no confidence in the flesh."

Philippians 3:3

"In whom also ye are circumcised with the circumcision made without hands, ***in putting off the body of the sins of the flesh*** by the circumcision of Christ:"

Colossians 2:11

We circumcise our heart by cutting off our "sin man", by denying our sin, and by telling him that he cannot flow out of our mouth(s), unless it is in confession of sin to God and Jesus.

"I will arise and go to my father, and will say unto him, *Father, I have sinned against heaven, and before thee.*"

Luke 15:18

"I acknowledge my sin unto thee, and mine iniquity have I not hid. I said, I will confess my transgressions unto the Lord; and thou forgavest the iniquity of my sin."

Psalm 32:5

I will tell you this up front: the first time you cut off your "sin man" and cast him out of your body; it will cause your heart, soul and feelings to hurt. You are used to defending yourself. Thus, it will take the power of Jesus to gain control over your mouth (**Mark 8:34 & John 17:1-2**)!!! Cutting into our flesh (our defensive feelings) *always hurts*!

"For in many things we offend all. *If any man offend not in word*, the same is a perfect man, and able also to bridle the whole body."

James 3:2

We are told to pluck out our "sin man's" eye; not our physical eye. And, we are told to cut off our "sin man's" hand or foot; not our physical hand or foot. We do these deeds by first realizing that we have a lustful desire to defend our sin that lives on the inside of us (**Psalm 32:5 & 36:1-2**). And secondly, we talk to our "sin man's" desire who lives on the inside of ourselves and tell it "NO" (**Matthew 16:24**)!

Once you start this, the "sin man" will tell your mind, "It is only crazy people who talk to themselves". This is not true! King David talked to his own soul all the time!

"And David was greatly distressed; for the people spake of stoning him, because the soul of all the people was grieved, every man for his sons and for his daughters: but David encouraged himself in the Lord his God."

I Samuel 30:6

"Why art thou cast down, O my soul? and why art thou disquieted in me? hope thou in God: for I shall yet praise him for the help of his countenance."

Psalm 42:5

"Why art thou cast down, O my soul? and why art thou disquieted within me? hope thou in God: for I shall yet praise him, who is the health of my countenance, and my God."

Psalm 42:11

If you take the time to read the entire forty second Psalm, you will see that King David is talking to himself (his soul) the whole Psalm. You need to open up your own mouth and speak over your own sin man. You need to be in control, not your sin!

When Jesus desired the fig tree to dry up and die, He had to open His mouth and speak over the tree in order for it to happen!

"And when he saw a fig tree in the way, he came to it, and found nothing thereon, but leaves only, ___and said unto it___, *Let no fruit grow on thee henceforward for* ever. And presently the fig tree withered away."

Matthew 21:19

Our power is in our **OWN tongue**!

> "Death and life are in the power of the tongue: and they
> that love it shall eat the fruit thereof."

Proverbs 18:21

And unless we open our mouths and speak over our own sin within
us, our flesh will always win! If we refuse to use our tongue in Jesus'
way, then the only other alternative is for us to lose, because our "old
man" will remain in control of our bodies.

Remember Saul? He refused to follow God's words; and because he
did, his fleshly desires won over his life (**I Samuel Ch. 15**).

> "Know ye not, that to whom ye yield yourselves servants to
> obey, his servants ye are to whom ye obey; whether of sin
> unto death, or of obedience unto righteousness?"

Romans 6:16

If you refuse to speak over your flesh and tell him "No", then this is
sin on your part because you are disobeying Jesus' words (**Matthew
16:24 & Mark 8:34**). You are disobeying; because unless you do
this act, you will defend yourself again (**Matthew 16:24-25 & John
8:34**). To complain because things are NOT going "YOUR WAY" or
defend yourself is always sin. This is because YOU are trying to exalt
your own self (your beliefs and the way that you see things as being
right) (**Proverbs 12:15**), over other people (**Luke 18:10-14**)!!

It doesn't matter if you are right as according to the scriptures, you
still cannot exalt yourself as being right. Jesus was right all the time.
But when His followers decided to stop following Him, in **John**

6:30-66, He didn't defend Himself. He let His believers go their own way and believe as they saw fit (**Matthew 16:24** & **Mark 8:34**). This doesn't mean that He agreed with the wrong people. He just let them choose their own destiny (**Matthew 15: 13-14**) Jesus did not defend Himself. If He did, it would have been sin.

So if you defend yourself, this would be in direct disobedience to Jesus' commandment in **Matthew 5:38; 16:24** & **Mark 8:34**. And to disobey Jesus' Words is to sin. Once you give into your sin, you are doomed to continue to serve your sin.

> "Jesus answered them, *Verily, verily, I say unto you, Whosoever committeth sin is the servant of sin.*"

> **John 8:34**

So, instead of serving our sin, our Master tells us to deny it and to speak to the mountain of sin which lies in our soul(s) and to cast it from us.

> "For verily I say unto you, That whosoever *shall say* unto this mountain, *Be thou removed, and be thou cast into the sea*; and shall not doubt in his heart, but shall believe that those things which he saith shall come to pass; he shall have whatsoever he saith."

> **Mark 11:23**

He also instructs us to do the SAME thing with our sin in **Matthew 5:29-30** & **18:7-9**. Didn't Jesus tell us to cut off our sin man and cast him from us?

"And if thy right eye offend thee, pluck it out, and cast it from thee: . . ."

Matthew 5:29A

"And if thy right hand offend thee, cut it off, and cast it from thee: . . ."

Matthew 5:30A

"Wherefore if thy hand or thy foot offend thee, cut them off, and cast them from thee: . . ."

Matthew 18:8A

"And if thine eye offend thee, pluck it out, and cast it from thee: . . ."

Matthew 18:9A

We are to speak to our "mountain of sin" and cast it away from us. This is the only way we are going to gain control over "him" (**Mark 11:23-24** & **John 8:34, 44**).

I will tell you again: the first time you deny your mouth (**Matthew 15:18-20** & **Mark 7:20-23**); you will feel uneasy in your spirit. Your sin (your mouth) has always won in the past. And it will not know what to do when you throw it off base for the first time.

You must train your mouth, before, you will begin to feel comfortable again (**James Ch. 3**). But in the end, your God-given Spirit will be stronger than your "sin man" (**Revelation 3:18-22**)! This will be GOOD: Very good (**Revelation Ch. 2-3**)!!

We have gone into a lot of facts in this chapter. It is time to close so you can look up the scriptures and meditate on Jesus' Words. Let the Holy Spirit burn this truth down into your conscious (heart(s)).

In our next chapter, we will go into more detail on **Mark 11:22-26**.

CHAPTER 25

Doing Jesus' Words IV

IN OUR LAST CHAPTER, the Holy Spirit showed us what Jesus was telling us to do in **Matthew 5:28-30; 18:7-9** and **Mark 9:43-48**. We are told by Him to cut off our "old man" and cast this mountain of sin out of our body. In these scriptures, Jesus doesn't call our sin a mountain. But if you will ask for the revelation knowledge; the Holy Spirit will begin to teach you. Because our sin is bigger and stronger than we are, our Savoir is referring to our sin as being the mountain in our lives.

Doesn't He tell us, we are servants to our "sin man" in **John 8:34**? When you are a servant, you serve your master. This means you are subject to your sin; he is not subject to you. In other words, you will obey him, instead of him obeying you (**John 8:44**). Therefore, because we cannot control our sin continuously, he is a mountain that we **cannot** handle. So, Jesus has given us a way to handle him.

> "And in the morning, as they passed by, they saw the fig tree dried up from the roots. And Peter calling to remembrance saith unto him, Master, behold, the fig tree which thou cursedst is withered away. And Jesus answering saith unto them, Have faith in God. For verily I say unto you, That whosoever shall say unto this mountain, Be thou removed, and be thou cast into the sea; and shall not doubt in his

heart, but shall believe that those things which he saith shall come to pass; he shall have whatsoever he saith."

Mark 11:20-23

Let's study this out. Remember, we are talking about our sin. As far as I can remember, there hasn't been a minister who has shown us the way in which God, Jesus and the Holy Spirit, deal with our sin in relationship back to God. So, the Holy Spirit is going to show you how to deal with your sin in this chapter.

There will be areas in which it will seem as if the Holy Spirit is repeating. Thus, you are going to have to be serious enough with God to go to Him and ask Him why. If you are sober (serious) enough, God will give you the revelation knowledge from His lesson.

Let's start with **Mark 11:14**. Have you ever seen a fig tree that doesn't bear fruit? It is ugly. This barren fig tree represents what our sin looks like to God. Let's get honest, our sin is ugly. Therefore, Jesus teaches us to get as strong against our sin as He did against the ugly tree. Our Master opened up His mouth and He cursed the tree.

> "And Jesus answered and said unto it, No man eat fruit of thee hereafter for ever. And his disciples heard it."

Mark 11:14

> "And when he saw a fig tree in the way, he came to it, and found nothing thereon, but leaves only, and said unto it, Let no fruit grow on thee henceforward for ever. And presently the fig tree withered away."

Matthew 21:19

Mark tells us that the disciples heard what Jesus told the tree. This means Jesus spoke His words loud enough for the people around Him to hear exactly what He said. Our Messiah was not meek and mild when He cursed the tree, which signified our sin.

The barren tree represents the man who does not bear the "fruits of the Spirit" unless it suits him (**John 15:1-6, 16; Matthew 7:15-20 & 12:33-37**). This kind of person is a perpetual sinner in God and Jesus' eyes (**Matthew 7:19; 12:33-37 & John 15:6**). This is because he doesn't know how to give the "fruits of the Spirit" constantly; and with love in his heart (**I Corinthians 13:1-8**).

He/she doesn't give compassion unless it suits him/her to do so (**Matthew 7:12 & Luke 6:31**). And, he/she is very selective in the way he/she gives mercy to other people (**James 2:13**).

He/she will give the mercy and kindness to the people who think the way he/she does. This is because it is suiting him/her to do so (**Matthew 5:46-48; & 9:11-13**). *He/she will also give the mercy to himself/ herself* because he/she always agrees with himself/herself (**Matthew Ch. 23**).

But when people do NOT agree with their views on life, it becomes hard for the fruitless people to give the mercy and compassion to their foes. Thus, they just will not do Jesus' Words in **Matthew 5:38-48**. This is why they are called fruitless by Jesus in **Matthew 13:22; 23:1-3; Mark 4:19** and **Luke 8:14**!

These people are compared to the fruitless fig tree in **Matthew 21:18-22** and **Mark 11:12-14**. The tree only gave fruit when it suited the tree to do so. And this is the way it is with Jesus' fruitless people. They only give the "fruits of the Spirit" when it suits them to do so. And because they are refusing to do Jesus' Words continually, at the times when they refuse to do His Words, they end up disobeying Him (**Matthew 5:38-48, 6:12, 14-15; 7:12; Luke 6:31** and **John 13:34; & 15:12-13**). When you don't do Jesus' Words, you cannot produce the "fruits of the Spirit" (**John 15:1-5**).

For example, when you refuse to give the mercy (forgiveness); compassion (gentleness, goodness) and love to your opponent, you are NOT producing the "fruits of the Spirit". Nor are you walking in the Spirit (**Romans 8:1**). *You MUST give the "fruits of the Spirit" continually* to be considered by God and Jesus to be the one who is walking in the Spirit (**Ezekiel 18:24 Matthew 6:22-24; 12:33-34 & Luke 16:1-13**).

In other words, YOU chose to give the "fruits of the Spirit" when it suits you (**Ezekiel 18:21; Matthew 7:12 & Luke 6:31**). And you can refuse to provide the "fruits of the Spirit" when it doesn't suit you (**Ezekiel 18:24; Matthew 7:12-20; 12:33-37; Luke 6:43-49; & James Ch. 3**). But if you give out the "fruits of the Spirit" in this way, you will not be considered by God and Jesus to be walking in the Spirit (**Galatians 5:14-26**). Thus, you are the one who is condemned in **Romans 8:1** and **James 2:13**!!

Remember, Jesus' blood doesn't cover your sins until you stop sinning and produce the "fruits of the Spirit" continuously (**John 3:19-21; 15:1-6, 16; Romans 8:1; Galatians 5:14-26; Hebrews 10:35-36; James 2:13 & I John 1:7**). In other words, Jesus' blood doesn't cover your sins until you repent. And **John 3:19-21** is what Jesus requires as your repentance!! **John 3:21** is what this book is all about!

You must give the mercy (forgiveness) continually in order to be able to receive it for yourself (**Matthew 6:12 & James 2:13**)!! And you MUST give—use—do the "fruits of the Spirit" all the time in order to be able to WALK in the Spirit (**Galatians 5:14-26**)!! When you do NOT, then you are the same as the barren fig tree (**Matthew 12:33-37**).

However, these instructions are impossible to do, unless you remove your "sin man" who has the rule over your life (**John 8:34; Matthew 19:26; Mark 10:27 & Luke 18:27**)!!

As the Holy Spirit showed us in His past lessons; if we refuse to do Jesus' Words written in His gospel, we will be disobeying our Master's Words (**John 12:48**)! And disobeying is sin.

> "And Samuel said, Hath the LORD as great delight in burnt offerings and sacrifices, as in obeying the voice of the LORD? Behold, to obey is better than sacrifice, and to hearken than the fat of rams. For rebellion is as the sin of witchcraft, and stubbornness is as iniquity and idolatry. Because thou hast rejected the word of the LORD, he hath also rejected thee from being king."
>
> **I Samuel 15:22-23**

When we choose to disobey Jesus' Words by NOT doing them, we are sinning (**Luke 6:46**), because we are rejecting Y'shua's Words (**John 12:48**). To reject Jesus' Words is the same sin as rebellion in God and Jesus' eyes. Read **I Samuel Ch. 15**. We do NOT possess the luxury of being able to choose when we want to do Jesus' Words and when we don't want to do them (**John 15:1-6**). This is what King Saul did in **I Samuel Ch. 15**. He was rejected by God and seen as a perpetual sinner because he was rebelling against God's Words by rejecting them. We were just told by Samuel in **I Samuel 15:22-23** that rebellion is the sin of witchcraft. And stubbornness is iniquity and idolatry.

We either DO Jesus' Words in our lives constantly, or we are sinning because we are rejecting them. We cannot sin and do Jesus' Words at the same time. It is physically impossible to do both (**Matthew 6:24** & **Luke 16:13**).

Thus, our Master shows us what God and He thinks about the man who is rejecting His Words by not doing them (**Luke 6:46**)!

Quite frankly, Jesus cursed the tree. And He is asking you to curse your sin who wants to rule (and is ruling) your life. He is asking you to do it in the same way as He cursed the tree.

Our Master tells us to say unto this mountain, "Be thou removed, and be thou cast into the sea".

Again, we are told, our sin is our mountain because it is bigger and stronger than we are and almost impossible to fight. Thus, we will give into our flesh when telling it "no" becomes hard to do.

So, Jesus tells us in **Mark 9:43-48; 11:23; Matthew 5:29-30** & **18:8-9** instead of trying to fight with him, we just cast this mountain of sin away from us and into the sea. And if we do not doubt these words in our hearts, then this mountain has to obey our voices.

> "For verily I say unto you, That whosoever shall say unto this mountain, Be thou removed, and be thou cast into the sea; and shall not doubt in his heart, but shall believe that these things which he saith shall come to pass; he shall have whatsoever he saith. Therefore I say unto you, What things soever ye desire, when ye pray, believe that ye receive them, and ye shall have them."

> **Mark 11:23-24**

There is one more command that the Holy Spirit is revealing to me. Before Jesus told the disciples to cast the mountain away from them, our Y'shua made it easy to remove the sin by first drying it up from the root.

Do you remember what Jesus did to the fig tree? He cursed it.

> "And Jesus answered and said unto it, No man eat fruit of thee hereafter for ever. And his disciples heard it."

> **Mark 11:14**

And the tree dried from the roots up to the top of it.

> "And in the morning, as they passed by, they saw the fig tree dried up from the roots."

> **Mark 11:20**

It would help us if we asked Jesus to dry up our sin from the root up to the top of our tree as well. This is so it will become easier to remove. (It is almost impossible to pull up and remove a living tree).

We must *stop sinning* completely, or be judged by Jesus as being the permanent sinner. This is because we are doing both the good and the bad from the SAME body (tree) (**Genesis 3:5; Matthew 7:15-19; 12:33; Luke 6:43-45; & James 3:8-18**). We do the good by producing Jesus' Words (**John 15:1-5**). We produce His Words by doing them when it suits us to do so (**Genesis 3:5; Matthew 12:33-37; Luke 6:46; John 15:1-5 & James 3:9-10**).

Then, Jesus' church people will turn around and judge (**Luke 6:41-45**); talk bad about other people (**Matthew 12:33-37; Luke**

6:42-45 & **James 3:8-17**); hold a grudge (**James 5:9**); complain because things are NOT working the WAY it suits THEM (**Numbers 13:27-14:10; & Jude 15-16**); think bad thoughts and do many other sins (**Matthew 15:18-20 & Mark 7:20-23**). By sinning from the same tree (the same body), the sins override the good that we have done (**Genesis 3:5; Ezekiel 18:24; Isaiah 64:6 Matthew 6:24; 12:35-37 & Luke 16:1-13**).

And then God sees us as only being the sinners we are (**Genesis 3:5; Isaiah 64:6 & Matthew 12:33-34**). Remember, Jesus' blood does NOT cover our sins until we complete **John 3:21 & I John 1:7**!! No matter what you think, your thoughts are NOT going to change what Jesus will do for you (**Matthew 25:1-12**)!!

It is better to stop sinning than to suffer the consequence of your sin. And it is simpler to stop when your sin man (your root of sin) is dead because you asked Jesus to curse it for you. When He did curse your root of sin, this act caused it to dry from the bottom of the roots up to the top of the tree (**Matthew 12:33**). It is less painful to cast a dead tree away than it is a living one (**Matthew 18:7-9**).

Now, you can stop sinning because your sin isn't in your body any longer to tempt you (**James 1:14**). But there is still one problem which can STOP your prayer of **Mark 11:23-24**. We will address this problem in our next chapter.

CHAPTER 26

Doing Jesus' Words V

S O FAR, WE HAVE studied the fact that we must deal with our sins personally and acknowledge them one at a time (**Psalm 32:5A & I John 1:8-10**). We must confess them out loud to God and Jesus (**Psalm 32:5B & I John 1:9**). We must ask Jesus if He will dry up the root of the sin (**Deuteronomy 30:5-6; Matthew 21:19-20; Mark 11:14, 20 & Colossians 2:11**). And then we must cast these things (sins) out by our mouths one at a time (**Matthew 5:29A, 30A; 18:8A, 9A; Mark 11:23-24 & Romans 2:26, 29**).

God and Jesus are very serious about Their instructions (**Deuteronomy 18:18-19; 28:1-2, 15; John 12:47-50 & Acts 3:23**). They will not forgive us unless we do Jesus' Words constantly (**Matthew 25:1-12; John 6:53-54, 56; I John 3:24; Romans 2:13; John 15:1-6 & Acts 3:23**). Once we do begin to complete Their commandments in our lives (**John 15:1-5**), we are on our way to God's forgiveness (**Psalm 32:5; Psalm 51**). But there is one problem which can still stand in our way. It is unforgiveness.

Doesn't Jesus tell us in **Mark 11:25-26**, if we refuse to forgive, then our prayer of **Mark 11:22-24** will **not** work? This means that it will work when we pray the prayer, _**but**_, if we don't go on and complete **Mark 11:25-26**, then our sin will return to our bodies again (**Luke 11:23-26**). Thus, our sins will NOT leave our body and _**stay gone**_ because **Mark 11: 22-24** did NOT work completely. God gives us grace by not allowing **Luke 11:23-26** to happen to us until we have worked though **Mark 11:25-26** (**Romans 6:1-2**).

Our Heavenly Father understands that forgiveness is impossible to do unless we have Jesus' help (**John 17:2**). Thus, there will be times when our sins will just remain in our bodies even though we are praying the **Mark 11:23-24** prayer. Remember, we MUST be serious, or God and Jesus' Words will NOT help us (**John 15:1-6**)! Let's study this out.

> "And Jesus answering saith unto them. Have faith in God. For verily I say unto you, That whosoever shall say unto this mountain, Be thou removed, and be thou cast into the sea; and shall not doubt in his heart, but shall believe that those things which he saith shall come to pass; he shall have whatsoever he saith. Therefore I say unto you, what things soever ye desire, when ye pray, believe that ye receive them, and ye shall have them. And when ye stand praying, *forgive*, if ye have ought against any: that your Father also which is in heaven may forgive you your trespasses. But if ye **_do not_** forgive, **_neither will your Father which is in heaven forgive your trespasses._**"

> Mark 11:22-26

If we were not serious enough to really want to do Jesus' Words by forgiving, God will not back up our prayer and our sins will remain. Since, we still have our sins; they will nag us to give into them (**John 8:34**). And more than likely, we will do it, because they are stronger than we are (**John 8:44**).

Once we sin again, we are NOW condemned (**Ezekiel 18:24; John 3:19-20 & 8:35**). Because we are SINNERS, we NEED God and Jesus' forgiveness (**Leviticus 17:11; Hebrew 9:19-22 & Matthew 26:27-28**). We CANNOT get into heaven without Jesus' salvation (**John Ch. 3**)!!! And you must remember; Jesus' salvation is HIS, to give to us!! We cannot demand our LORD to give it to us! Thus, if He tells us that God will NOT forgive us of our sins, if we refuse to forgive the ones who sinned against us, then HE means what He has said!!! Thus, we are doomed to stay in our sins if we do NOT forgive Jesus' way (**Matthew 5:19A, 22-26; 6:12; 14-15; 18:21-35; Mark 11:25-26; Luke 12:49-59; 16:19-25; John 8:21, 23-24 & James 2:13**).

Read Y'shua's Words from your heart: not your head. He tells us outright if we refuse to forgive the people who have hurt us; then neither will God forgive us for the things we have done against Him and other people (**Mark 11:25-26**).

Why would Jesus tell us this at the end of His/our prayer? Remember what we are praying in **Mark 11:22-24**? We are confessing our sin and casting it off and out of our bodies so that God can forgive us for sinning. We need this forgiveness if we are going to stay out of hell. This is plain and simple. Sin requires the payment of hell.

"The soul that sinneth, it shall die."

Ezekiel 18:20A

"For the wages of sin is death; . . ."

Romans 6:23A

Therefore, in order for us to be able to keep God's forgiveness in our lives, we must do Jesus' Words in **Mark 11:25-26**.

> "(For **not** the hearers of the law are just before God, but the *doers of the law* shall be justified."

> **Romans 2:13**

Since we have realized we MUST do Jesus' Words or end our lives in hell (**Matthew 25:31-46**), then *we will* get serious enough to be determined to forgive, and then God will back up our prayer when we pray it. Presently we have gotten rid of sin (**Mark 11:22-24**), and our vessel is empty. We NEED to fill it back up again or Satan will take advantage of our empty bodies.

> "When the unclean spirit is gone out of a man, he walketh through dry places, seeking rest; and finding none, he saith, I will return unto my house whence I came out. And when he cometh, he findeth it swept, and garnished. Then goeth he, and taketh to him seven other spirits more wicked than himself; and they enter in, and dwell there: and the last state of that man is worse than the first."

> **Luke 11:24-26**

We fill our house (our bodies) back up by DOING Jesus' Words. Remember the root (the promise of God)? It grows when we continue to DO Jesus' Words (**Matthew 6:33**). We do not want to lose what we have gained (**I Corinthians 9:24-27; Hebrew 10:35 & 12:1C**). We have come this far, let's continue on, because we must go all the way to the end, or again we will lose all that we have worked for (**Galatians 6:9 & Hebrews 10:36**). We have worked for our reward, *NOT our salvation*!

"For the Son of man shall come in the glory of his Father with his angels; and then he shall REWARD every man ACCORDING TO HIS WORKS."

Matthew 16:27

Our works only put us in the position where Jesus can give us our salvation (**Hebrews 10:36**)! Do you remember what we were told? When we DO Jesus' Words (God's Law) these acts put us in the position for Jesus to be able to justify us (**James 2:19-26**). It is the doers of the law that Jesus justifies, not the hearers (**Romans 2:13**).

"Cast *not away* therefore your confidence, which hath great recompence of **reward**. For ye have need of patience, that, after ye have done the will of God, *ye might receive* the promise."

Hebrew 10:35-36

But, if we *refuse* to *do* God's law: then we *cannot* even be put in the position to become justified by Jesus (**Matthew 5:17-19; 19:16-22; Mark 10:17-22; Luke 18:18-23; Romans 2:13 & Revelation 22:14**).

It is only the ones who are willing to go all the way to the end who are allowed to receive the *good* rewards (**I Corinthians 3:9-15**). Read Jesus' Words in **Revelation Ch. 2 & 3**. It is ONLY the Christian that overcomes ALL, who receives the *good* rewards!!

So let's go on. We have worked this hard. Let's finish the race (**I Corinthians 9:24-27**). Let's go on and find out what we must do to be able to forgive in Jesus' way.

"And when ye stand praying, ___forgive___, if ye have ought against any: _that your Father also which is in heaven may forgive you your trespasses_. But if ye do not forgive, neither will your Father which is in heaven forgive your trespasses."

Mark 11:25-26

We will study this truth out in our next lesson.

CHAPTER 27

Forgiveness

I N THESE NEXT SEVERAL lessons, we are going to study how we are to forgive in the way Jesus teaches us to forgive (**John 14:6**). We can tell ourselves we have forgiven our offenders. But the Holy Spirit through our consciousness will let us know if we did or if we didn't.

From this point on, the Holy Ghost is going to make this personal. He will be talking to you personally, because He has already taught me Jesus' way of forgiving. I had to follow His instructions or, I would be right where you may be now.

You see, if you really have forgiven from the bottom of your heart, the following words will NOT offend you. But if you haven't, the upcoming teachings may be very offensive to you. If you are interested you can read on.

The Holy Spirit lets you know that there is still a problem between God, Jesus, your wrongdoer and yourself by bringing the situation which offended you into your mind.

When this event does enter into your mind, do all the SAME old feelings come flooding back to your intellect again? Are you still upset because of the way you were treated? Sometimes the situation will pop into your mind from time to time. And sometimes, the event that was so offensive to you personally, will return to your mind quite often. This is the Holy Spirit letting you know the situation between your offender and yourself is not over.

Didn't Jesus tell us one of the works the Holy Spirit will do is to reprove us of the sin we have committed, of righteousness, and of judgment?

> "And when he is come, he will reprove the world of sin, and of righteousness, and of judgment: Of sin, because they believe not on me; Of righteousness, because I go to my Father, and ye see me no more; Of judgment, because the prince of this world is judged."

John 16:8-11

This means, the Holy Spirit will reprove anyone (Christian or not) of sin, of righteousness and of judgment. The proof of this statement is this: There are Christians which will call the ministers and tell them they are worried because they don't feel saved. Or the Christians will tell the minister they don't feel forgiven. Or they will tell the minister they are uneasy about a situation which may be going on in their lives.

All these situations are the Holy Spirit dealing with the Christians (**John 16:8-11**). He is trying to reveal to these people that there are problems between them and God. This is **John 16:8-11** taking place in the born-again people's lives.

It would be good for the believers to listen to what the Holy Spirit is trying to tell them. If they don't, Jesus and God will let them go in their own direction (**Romans 1:17-32; Isaiah 57:17; Matthew**

7:26-27; 15:13-14 & **Luke 6:46, 49**). And they will end up failing. In God and Jesus' eyes, they are failing because they are rebelling against God and Jesus' Words (**Psalm 81:13-14; Matthew 15:1-14; John 16:8-11** & **I Samuel 15:18-23**).

This is what our Lord meant when He said in **John 16:9** "Of sin, because they believe ***not*** on me:"

Jesus is telling us in this verse that the people who are being reprimanded by the Holy Spirit do ***not*** believe on Him. They do not believe on the Lord Jesus Christ, because *they are calling the minister and believing the minister's words, instead of listening to the Holy Spirit who is working through their own consciousness.* The Christians are **NOT listening** to their God-given Spirit which lives on the inside of them (**John 16:8-11** & **12:48**). And unless they start paying attention to the Holy Spirit's convictions, there is no forgiveness for the sin (**I Samuel Ch. 15** & **Luke 13:1-5**).

Let's study this situation out so we can understand. Again the Holy Spirit is going to get personal. You need to know, He will bring the same event up to your mind all over again because this is the way He causes us to meditate. When He does bring up the incident, He will then teach you what you need to know so you can learn how to conquer your circumstance.

Let's say the Holy Spirit brings a memory to mind of a person who offended you. In your mind, the event happened all over again and all your old feelings resurfaced to your conscience just the same as if the occurrence had just happened. You are STILL offended and upset at what took place and you wish that it never happened. Because you were never taught that this is the Holy Spirit dealing with you personally, you pick up the phone and call your minister. You tell him you are still troubled. You also tell him sometimes you don't feel as if you are saved.

Your minister will ask you if you prayed the sinner's prayer. If you tell him you did, then he will reassure you that all is okay.

But the situation will continue to nag your awareness. You believe your minister. Therefore, when the event enters your mind again and again, you tell yourself all is okay with God and yourself. You decide to fight your own consciousness to the point you actually believe all is okay and you become comfortable with yourself.

Because of your minister's words, you were not aware that the nagging was actually the Holy Spirit still dealing with you personally about the offensive event. And because you didn't understand, this was the Holy Spirit who was pulling at your heart; you fought your awareness until you won your battle over your mind.

You don't know it, but you have actually told the Holy Spirit to leave you alone. You have told Him you know you are saved and you have forgiven your offender whether you believe this statement or not. Therefore, the Holy Ghost will remain quiet and leave you alone. This is God, Jesus and the Holy Ghost allowing you to go your way (**Romans 1:18-32** & **Psalm 81:10-12**).

This is you believing your minister's words over Jesus' Words. Remember? He told us in **John 16:8-9** that the Holy Spirit would reprove us of *our sins*, because we do not believe on Him. This is what He means! Because we have NOT been taught that the Holy Spirit would reprove the Christian world of their sins, it is easier to believe the ministers' words instead of Jesus' Words in **John 16:8-9**. This is why we do NOT believe on Him!

Remember what **Isaiah 5:13** and **Hosea 4:6** tells us? We will be destroyed for lack of knowledge. This means we are destroyed for lack of revelation knowledge.

Now you are in a bad situation. You have not really forgiven your offender because you didn't listen to your consciousness. And because you have NOT forgiven your offender, in Jesus' eyes (not your own) you are not forgiven by God. (Remember? In your eyes all is well.) But all is NOT well in Jesus' eyes, and this is why you cannot feel as if you are saved.

> "But if ye forgive NOT men their trespasses, neither will your Father forgive your trespasses."

Matthew 6:15

This situation is NOT really your fault and neither is it the minister's. Your pastor is just telling you what He has been taught by his mentors. It takes us being willing to break away from our teachings and allow the Holy Ghost to deal with us personally to be able to understand God and Jesus' viewpoints on the scriptures.

Remember? Revelation knowledge is the ONLY kind of knowledge which the gates of hell cannot prevail against (**Matthew 16:18-19**). And because this fact is true, the gates of hell can and do prevail against information that comes from our ministers, if their data is not from God's revealed knowledge.

As a result of NOT operating our lives from God's revelation knowledge, the gates of hell prevail over the information which comes from man's own knowledge. And this knowledge causes us to fall.

Remember? This is what happened to Adam and Eve when they ate the fruit from the tree of good and evil in **Genesis 2:17 & 3:1-6.** Adam fell from living on God's revelation knowledge to living on and from information that comes from man's own thinking (**Proverbs 16:2, 25**). No one can name all the animals of the world from their own mind, not even Adam (**Genesis 2:19-20**). He received the names from God's revealed knowledge (**Matthew 16:17**).

When Adam ate the fruit, he could not receive any more of God's revealed knowledge (**Matthew 13:17**). This is what caused him and Eve to die (**Proverbs 14:12**). Satan was now allowed to give Adam and Eve his knowledge of evil and good (**Genesis 3:1-5**). This is what the tree of knowledge of good and *evil* is. Remember, when Satan was tempting Jesus in the wilderness? He quoted both a part of the truth from the Old Testament and lies as well (**Matthew 4:3, 5-6 & 8-9**). This partial quote was taken from **Psalm 91:11-12.**

Satan also knew if Jesus was God's Son, then He could change stones into bread (**Matthew 14:18-21**). And he knew, if Jesus was God's Son, then offering Him all the kingdoms of the world would also tempt Jesus, because the kingdoms were Satan's to offer (**Genesis 3:6 & Romans 5:12**). Without revelation knowledge no one would understand this reality in **Matthew 4:1-11** or any of the other scriptures from God and Jesus' viewpoint (**Isaiah 55:7-11 Matthew 11:29; 13:10-19 & 16:13-19**).

Therefore, one of the reasons Jesus came to this world, was to give God's revelation knowledge back to His people so they could survive (**Matthew 13:10-17 & 16:17-19**).

Remember, it is ONLY God's revealed knowledge that the gates of hell cannot prevail against. Thus, without this knowledge, there is NO way you can come out from under failure (**Matthew 16:18**).

You must repent (**Luke 13:1-5**). You need to ask God to forgive you for not paying attention to the Holy Spirit's rebuking; and decide to listen to Him instead of your minister (**John 16:8-11**). You need to ask if the Holy Spirit will return to your mind and begin to teach you again (**John 16:8-15**).

This will NOT happen overnight. You must study to show yourself approved (**II Timothy 2:15**). You must prove to your great cloud of witnesses you are faithful to study (**Hebrew 12:1**).

And eventually the Holy Spirit will begin to deal with you again. And guess what? Do you remember the event that upset you a while back? The picture of this offense will return to your mind again. This means the Holy Spirit is letting you know that there is STILL a problem between God, Jesus, your offender and yourself. This also means that there is STILL unforgiveness in your heart.

Now that you understand God and Jesus viewpoints on Their own Words, the Holy Spirit will begin to teach you how to forgive in Jesus' way in our next few lessons.

CHAPTER 28

Jesus' Forgiveness I

I N OUR LAST CHAPTER the Holy Spirit showed us how we can know if there is still unforgiveness in our hearts. In this lesson He is going to demonstrate how Jesus instructed us to forgive the unsaved people.

> "Ye have heard that it hath been said, An eye for an eye, and a tooth for a tooth: But I say unto you, That ye resist NOT evil: but whosoever shall smite thee on thy right cheek, turn to him the other also. And if any man will sue thee at the law, and take away thy coat, let him have thy cloke also. And whosoever shall compel thee to go a mile, go with him twain. Give to him that asketh thee, and from him that would borrow of thee turn not thou away".

Matthew 5:38-42

When you are out in public, there will be people who will offend you in one way or another. There will be people who will be mean and rude. Like the older gentlemen in the grocery store, they can push you out of their way. They can take your basket by mistake but never apologize for doing so. They can say that you are too close to them in line. The insensitive treatments could go on and on. This type of thing can happen any time you go anywhere in public. What does Jesus tell us to do if we are treated in this manner?

> "Ye have heard that it hath been said, An eye for an eye, and a tooth for a tooth: But I say unto you, That ye resist _NOT evil_: but whosoever shall smite thee on thy right cheek, turn to him the other also."

Matthew 5:38-39

In other words, Jesus tells us that the acts are EVIL. It would have been better for the person if he had NOT offended you.

> "Woe unto the world because of offences! for it must needs be that offences come; but woe to that man by whom the offence cometh."

Matthew 18:7

But the offenses are in the world to cause our OWN sins to surface into our minds. Remember who sends the offenses to us?

> "Think not that I am come to send peace on earth: I came not to send peace, but a sword."

Matthew 10:34

> "I am come to send fire on the earth; . . ."

Luke 12:49A

> "And the tongue is a fire, a world of iniquity: so is the tongue among our members, that it defileth the whole

body, and setteth on fire the course of nature; and it is set
on fire of hell."

James 3:6

"Suppose ye, that I am come to give peace on earth? I tell
you, Nay; but rather division:"

Luke 12:51

The bitter words and offenses, not only set our heart(s) on fire, but
divide up Jesus' family of God. Remember why He came to send us
these offenses?

"But he that received the seed into stony places, the same
is he that heareth the word, and anon with joy receiveth it;
Yet hath he not root in himself, but dureth for a while: *for
when tribulation or persecution ariseth because of the word*,
by and by he is offended."

Matthew 13:20-21

Remember, Jesus tells us in **Matthew 13:21** and in **Mark 4:17** that the
Christian is offended (persecuted) for the WORD'S sake. This is the
same as being persecuted for righteousness' sake in **Matthew 5:10**.

Remember what happens to us when we get offended? Most of our
sin feelings rise to the surface of our minds. We can know that we are
resenting because we are offended! Jesus wants us to deny ourselves
of allowing the sin feelings to come out of our mouths while we are in
public (**Matthew 16:24** & **Mark 8:34**).

But then after we go home, ask the Holy Spirit to bring back all of our feelings we had when we were offended and confess them to God. Use the offense to help you rid your body of the offensive feelings you had at the store or in the public place.

This is why Jesus has us offended for the Word's sake. He wants us to use the offenses to bring up our sin feelings and confess them to God and Himself. This is step one of purging our sins from our bodies (**John 15:1-3**).

Do you remember Jesus' Words in **Matthew 18:7-9**? He told us in these verses, if we are offended; then we are to cast out of our bodies the parts which are offended.

> "Wherefore if thy hand or thy foot offend thee, cut them off, and cast them from thee: it is better for thee to enter into life halt or maimed, rather than having two hands or two feet to be cast into everlasting fire. And if thine eye offend thee, pluck it out, and cast it from thee: it is better for thee to enter into life with one eye, rather than having two eyes to be cast into hell fire."

Matthew 18:8

In other words, if you have been offended by another person because he/she hurt your feelings, this usually means that it is your sin man who has been offended. And it is your sin man who Jesus is telling you to cut off and cast away from you. It is the sin which lives on the inside of your body who has offended you and your God-given Spirit because he/she has gone against Jesus' Words by demanding that he/she is right. And he/she wants his/her offender to apologize and make things right.

"For whosoever exalteth himself shall be abased; and he that humbleth himself shall be exalted."

Luke 14:11

These are the kind of feelings Jesus wants you to go home and confess to God and Him. Now the offended person is beginning to get honest with God and himself.

If you are having trouble identifying your personal feelings, ask Jesus to help you bring your feelings up to the surface of your mind. Humbly ask Him to help you to recognize the way you are feeling, and to reveal to you why the harsh treatment hurt your feelings. Wait for the Holy Spirit to start illuminating to you all your hurt feelings.

As they begin to surface into your mind and you do recognize them as being hurt feelings from your past, confess these feelings to God. Then ask Jesus for the strength to cast them away (**Matthew 5:29-30; 18:7-9 & Mark 11:23-24**).

If you are still wanting to feel sorry for yourself and you are really having a hard time casting away your sin feelings; ask Jesus to dry up the root of the feelings (**Mark 11:12-21**). Then do as He tells us to do to the mountain. Cast the mountain of sin into the sea (**Mark 11:21-24**).

Are you beginning to understand why we are offended for the Word's sake? It is so we can become hurt. Once we are offended, search out why. As the answers start to enter into our minds, this is the chance to allow ourselves to become honest with ourselves (**Psalm 32:5 & Luke 15:17-21**). Once we recognize this fact, we can use this occasion to confess these feelings to God and Jesus (**I John 1:9**).

Now that YOUR sin is gone, be sure to forgive your offender (**Mark 11:25-26**). Again, if you still cannot find it in your heart to forgive him/her; raise your hands to heaven and ask God to do the forgiving through you.

There is one more step that needs to be done. Do you remember Jesus' teaching in **Matthew 5:23-25**? He said if YOU did anything to cause a person to be angry at YOU, then you need to ask that person to forgive you.

Let's study this out. You were offended and resented the person who offended YOU, right? If you would have told the person that you were offended at him/her, would he/she tell you "it's all good, go your way"? Most likely they WOULDN'T. He/she would be offended at the fact that you didn't let him get away with the evil.

Now, in your heart, you have done a deed that has offended him/her, even though they do not know it. But your cloud of witnesses does know that you offended the other person. Now what are you going to do about the situation? You cannot find the person so you could apologize to him or her. And he wouldn't know what you are talking about if you did, because he doesn't know what he did to offend you.

The Holy Spirit will help you out. If you will just ask the person out loud to forgive you for being offended at him, then the Holy Spirit will take care of the matter.

As an example, you could say out loud, "Person in the store who offended me, I forgive you for offending me. And I ask you to forgive me for being offended at you for hurting my feelings. I am asking God to make it right. I pray in Jesus' name, amen". Remember, this is only an example.

I do not know how the Holy Spirit makes it right, but HE DOES!! Remember, He is a Spirit. And Spirits are NOT confined to time and space. Therefore, He can do things in the Spirit world that we cannot. This is how you leave your gift at the altar: go and be reconciled to the person, and then come again and ask God to accept you.

> "Therefore if thou bring thy gift to the altar, and there rememberest that thy brother hath ought against thee; Leave there thy gift before the altar, and go thy way; first be reconciled to thy brother, and then come and offer thy gift."

> **Matthew 5:23-24**

This is also how you turn the other cheek for your offender (**Matthew 5:39**).

This kind of forgiveness is fairly easy to do. You need to know, the rest is going to cost you. Jesus requires a payment to be made because we gave into our sins and sinned.

The teachers are WRONG when they tell us; there is NO payment YOU must give for your sins. Sins have a price. Jesus only took the chastisement of our peace away from us, not ALL of our punishment. Turn to **Isaiah 53:5** and read what part of OUR *chastisement* was laid on Him. The rest of our punishment belongs to us!! Did you know, there are 104 scriptures which tell us we will be punished for our sins?

> "But he was wounded for our transgressions, he was bruised for our iniquities: *the chastisement of our peace was upon him*; and with his stripes we are healed."

> **Isaiah 53:5**

"For, lo, I begin to bring evil on the city which is called by my name, and should ye be utterly unpunished? Ye shall NOT be unpunished: for I will call for a sword upon ALL THE INHABITANTS of the earth, saith the Lord of Hosts"

Jeremiah 25:29

Did you know the word Christian has the word CHRIST in the name? Therefore, the born again Christian of the New Testament is called by Jesus' name. Also, when the Holy Spirit has said the ___*Lord of hosts*___ will call the sword upon all the inhabitants of the earth, He means the born again Christian of the New Testament is included in this punishment (**Matthew 10:34**)!! You are a part of all the inhabitants of the earth!! All people will be punished by the sword, New Testament Christian, or not (**Jeremiah 25:29** & **Matthew 10:34**). Let's study some of our payment for our sins in the next chapter.

"For the time is come that judgment MUST begin at the house of God: and if it first begins at us, what shall the end be of them that obey not the gospel of God?"

I Peter 4:17

CHAPTER 29

Jesus' Forgiveness II

I N OUR LAST LESSON the Holy Spirit showed us how we are to deal with the people who offend us just in passing. More times than not, we will probably never come across their paths again. But this time Jesus is going to explain how we are to forgive _unbelievers_ who are involved in our lives. They may be our neighbors; we may have to work with them; they may end up being our friends; we have them in our children's lives at school and/or they are just in our everyday lives.

My family and I have already lived through this part of forgiveness and paid our heavy price in these areas. Jesus tells us (1) if we have paid our price; (2) if we have learned our lesson and (3) if we know how to forgive from the bottom of our hearts; then there is NO reason to have to live through the SAME lessons over and over again (**John 15:3**).

So again the Holy Spirit is going to write to YOU personally. These lessons only pertain to the people who really want to grow with Jesus.

If you have lived through Jesus' teachings and have grown up with and in Him (and you know you have forgiven all) then this will be a witness of what you have lived through. Now, let's go into an explanation of Jesus' lesson in **Matthew 5:40-44.**

Let's say there was a Christian family who lived in an older duplex next to a lady who was NOT a Christian. Some of the older duplexes have thinner walls and they can be more affordable than the newer homes. Money was one of the reasons the family moved into their side of the building. Being older, the lady next door had lived in her duplex for a while and she wasn't interested in moving. Neither did she want any part of God, nor was she interested in giving out any kindness.

The Christian family irritated the lady because they had children who liked to just be kids. They would run and play in their home just as children do. And because this lady lived close to the family, she could hear the children play through the walls.

She would complain about every little thing that went on next door. For example, if you would run the vacuum or washing machine too late, she would complain about that. If you talked too loud or too late, she would complain. And the list could go on and on. This lady couldn't have the family evicted because they stayed within the complex rules, but not hers. In other words, it would be hard to live in their home. The family couldn't move, because this was the ONE home they could afford. What do they do?

The first thing this husband and wife need to do is to go to God together as a couple. The Holy Spirit realizes that the non-Christian will go more against the wife and children, than the husband. But if the husband doesn't get involved and help out his wife, the situation could get worse. What does Jesus tell us in Matthew?

> "And if any man will sue thee at the law, and take away thy coat, let him have thy cloke also."

Matthew 5:40

You see, the Christian world doesn't realize it, but we are in a WAR. We are God's soldiers (**Joel 2:1-11**). And if we don't fight back against the war that is charging against us, we WILL lose. A soldier that doesn't defend himself loses the battle (**Joel 2:1-11**). Even the children comprehend this much.

But the Christian world doesn't understand the way that God and Jesus want them to fight back against the oncoming rage which is charging against them. If they fight back with the physical weapons, again, they will lose.

> "Then said Jesus unto him, Put up again thy sword into his place: for all they that take the sword shall perish with the sword."

> **Matthew 26:52**

> "He that leadeth into captivity shall go into captivity: he that killeth with the sword must be killed with the sword. Here is the patience and the faith of the saints."

> **Revelation 13:10**

So if we are told to fight back and yet we are NOT allowed to fight back in the way we KNOW, how are we going to defend ourselves?

We do this with the SAME weapon that Jesus used to defeat Satan. With LOVE! If you don't CHOOSE to pick up love and put it in your heart, you will never learn how to love. Love is a choice. It is not a feeling. It does NOT come into your body automatically. God and Jesus cannot put it in your heart *against your will*. And people cannot survive without it.

Look at all the people who live in the nations that are against God and Jesus. They are dying because there is NO LOVE in their hearts to help one another.

If you DON'T choose to love, it will be very hard to DO Jesus' commandments (**I Corinthians 13:1-3**). It is LOVE that softens the heart. It is LOVE that encourages the Christian to continue in their work of doing good actions. And it is LOVE that defeats the WAR that is raging against us.

When there is love in your heart, it will cause you to see the older lady with a different heart. Instead of being upset because of all the things that she is doing against you, fight back by loving her from God's kind of love.

> "But I say unto you, LOVE your enemies, bless them that curse you, do good to them that hate you, and pray for them which despitefully use you, and persecute you;"

Matthew 5:44

Let's return to the family. As was said before, the HUSBAND and wife need go to God together. They need to tell God the problems they are having with their neighbor. They need to tell Him that right now they cannot afford to move, so they are asking Him to please help them make peace with the lady (**Proverbs 16:7**). They also, need to ask God if He would please SHOW them the right way to approach their neighbor (**Proverbs 21:1**).

This is a warning up front—this may take some of your time. Again, you must prove to your great cloud of witnesses you are sincere and you are determined in your heart and mind that YOU are going to complete this step in your life (**Hebrews 12:1**). In other words, in your heart and mind YOU ARE GOING TO LEARN HOW TO LOVE, NO MATTER WHAT (**I Corinthians 13:1-8**). Do you see God's promise to you in **I Corinthians 13:8**?

"Charity NEVER faileth: . . ."

I Corinthians 13:8A

In other words, you defeat your foe with love that flows from your heart towards your enemy. If you are having a hard time doing this, then again; raise your hands towards heaven and ask God to give you HIS love. And ask Him if he will LOVE the lady through you (**Matthew 19:26** & **Luke 1:37**).

But do NOT forget to confess the bad feelings you have towards the lady. One of the main reasons that you have fallen into this trap is because there are other types of sins in your heart. And these sins need to rise into your mind.

Remember, the main reason we are sent offenses is to cause our sins to rise into our minds so we can confess them to God (**Matthew 18:7-9**). We have years of different sins which have entered into our hearts and minds. And just one time of being offended and confessing is NOT going to clear all of our sins out of our hearts all at once.

"I Am the true vine, and my Father is the husbandman. Every branch in me that beareth not fruit he taketh away: *and every branch that beareth fruit, he purgeth it, that it may bring forth MORE fruit*. Now ye are clean through the word which I have spoken unto you."

John 15:1-3

Jesus tells us that He will purge the sins out of our bodies time and time again so WE can bring forth MORE fruit and become a clean vessel for our Savior (**John 15:1-3; Ephesians 5:27** & **Philippians 3:21**). This means He will offend us over and over again so our sins will rise into our minds. This is so we can confess them and rid our bodies of them each time we are offended.

If we will be faithful to do this step every time we are offended, eventually our bodies will be cleared of all of our flesh sins!! This is why Jesus tells us in **John 15:3** that we are NOW clean through the Word which He has spoken!!

If we will stop and recognize we are offended so we can purge our bodies of our sins, we will have a huge understanding from God's world. Each time we become offended, we can stop, and ask God to show us what sin it is we need to confess. If we confess our sins each time we are offended, (which is clearing our bodies of sins), we can become clean in no time (**John15:1-3**)!

You see, there does come a time when the offenses do STOP attacking us. This is how we can know that we are clean from the inside out.

Let's return to the lady. The Holy Spirit may let you know that she is lonely. If He does, He may impress you to invite her to dinner some time. You may be impressed to take some time out of your busy schedule to talk with her. You may be impressed to give her a present at Christmas time. You may be impressed to have your children make friends with her by telling her good morning and good evening. Or the Holy Spirit may impress the children to make a gift for her. This is DOING Jesus' Words in **Matthew 5:44**. This is going out of your way to make improvements with the relationship before it gets worse.

Yes, it is going to cost you some love from your heart. This is giving your extra coat (**Matthew 5:40**). Doing these deeds is going to cost you some of your time; this is going the extra mile for the lady (**Matthew 5:41**). It is going to cost you some of your money; this is giving the gift and not asking for anything in return (**Matthew 5:42**). It is going to cost you some of your love (**Matthew 5:7, 44-48 & I Corinthians 13:1-8**). But doing these deeds is a lot easier than ending up with the BIG arguments that can end in disasters (**Psalm 81:13-15; Matthew 5:40 & I Corinthians 6:1**).

There are several reasons we have to live through these types of experiences. The first is to cause our sins to surface into our minds (**II Corinthians 10:4-3**). The second is to cause us to recognize our own sins (**Luke 15:17A**). The third is to confess our sins and purge our bodies by casting the sins off (**I John 1:9 & Matthew 18:7-9**). And the fourth is to teach us how to love and forgive our enemies (**Matthew 5:38-44 & 6:14-15**).

There is a warning. When we are dealing with non-Christians, ask God to be in control on the loving side. We can swing over and pour out TOO much love to the world's people. We only do what the Holy Spirit impresses us to do. If we are NOT impressed, do NOT do any more for the lady. Jesus gives us a warning.

> "Give NOT that which is holy unto the dogs, neither cast ye your pearls before swine, lest they trample them under their feet, and turn again and rend you."

> **Matthew 7:6**

Our LORD tells us to ASK before we act.

"Ask, and it shall be given you; seek, and ye shall find; knock, and it shall be opened unto you: For every one that asketh receiveth; and he that seeketh findeth; and to him that knocketh it shall be opened."

Matthew 7:7-8

In out next lessons, the Holy Spirit is going to demonstrate to us how we are to learn to LOVE and FORGIVE each other. This means He is going to illustrate how we are to LOVE and FORGIVE the Christian world.

CHAPTER 30

Jesus' Forgiveness III

I N OUR LAST TEACHING, we were warned in **Matthew 7:6-7** to be careful how we complete our commandment in **Matthew 5:38-44**. Most of our training in this scripture is for our true believers only.

We need to be taught how to love and forgive our family members inside of God so God can forgive us (**John 13:34**). Jesus tells us in **Matthew 6:14-15; 18:28-35** and in **Mark 11:25-26**, if we *refuse* to forgive our offenders, then God CANNOT forgive us for offending Him. Keep in mind, what we sow, we must reap. Therefore, if we sow unforgiveness, then we MUST reap God's unforgiveness (**Galatians 6:7-8** & **James 2:13**). And without God's forgiveness, we do end our lives in hell (**Matthew 18:21-35** & **Romans 6:23**). So, we are going to learn this forgiveness from Jesus' instructions.

Our LORD first tells us to return love for the hateful deeds that our offenders may have done to us. For example, there are wives who call the ministries because their husbands are alcoholics or into pornographic materials on the internet. These men have given their spouses a hard time.

Thus, the wives have a big stumbling block that they need to overcome if they want to be forgiven (**Romans 14:13**). This means, if they want God to forgive them, then they MUST learn how to forgive their husbands, whether they want to or not. Jesus shows us how to forgive them in **Matthew 5:44**.

> "Ye have heard that it hath been said, Thou shalt love thy neighbour, and hate thine enemy. But I say unto you, ***Love you enemies***, . . ."

Matthew 5:43-44A

Our first training is to put LOVE in our hearts for our offenders. If we do NOT choose to do this act on purpose, the rest of these instructions will be very hard to complete (**I Corinthians 13:1-8**).

Choosing to receive LOVE into our hearts is one of the most important things we must learn to do. It is almost impossible to function in the Christian world without it, because without the LOVE, everything we do is labored. Without love, we are forcing ourselves to do the good deeds instead of wanting to do them. And this act causes our hearts to labor when we must do the Spirit's fruits (**Matthew 11:28-30**)!!

Let's return to our example. When your husband doesn't show up for dinner and you want to throw the dinner out, don't!! Stop yourself in midstream of all your activities and go to God in prayer!! Confess the bad feelings you are having towards your husband (**I John 1:9**). And rid your heart of the sins the situation is causing you to have (**Matthew 18:7-9**). If your resentment and bitterness is strong, remember to ask Jesus to dry up the roots of your sins so they can be removed easier (**Mark 11:12-24**).

Now that you are clean in this area of your life (**John 15:1-3**); you must fill your empty heart back up (**Matthew 12:43-44**). You do this deed by doing the "fruits of the Spirit" with LOVE in your heart (**Matthew 5:44**). If you choose NOT to do the Spirit's fruits with love, then the demon who left will return with seven more demons because your heart will remain empty (**Matthew 12:45; & Luke 11:17-26**). Jesus tells us, if this happens, you will be worse off than before you prayed (**Matthew 12:45C & Luke 11:26**).

So, on purpose, put the dinner away and surprise your husband. Get up when he does come home and heat up the dinner and serve it to him with a smile. Do not question him or complain because he wasn't home to eat with you. This is returning love for the hate he has put you through. Set with him and have a cup of tea or coffee while he eats. Say nothing, but gather up the dishes and put them into the sink and just go back to bed.

The Holy Spirit does realize how hard this act is to do. He does know about the housework, children, obligations, and jobs that are looking you in the face.

But, stop and think about your future. If you do NOT do something to replace your resentment, it could most definitely return to you seven times stronger (**Luke 11:17-26**). And if you cannot keep it out of your heart, you are looking at hell after death (**Matthew 5:21-26; 6:14-15; 18:22-35; Mark 11:25-26 & Luke 12:57-59**).

Remember what Jesus tells us? If we cannot overcome our hate, resentment, bitterness, anger, and/or bad thoughts; this is sin that is lingering in our hearts (**Matthew 15:18-20 & Mark 7: 20-23**). It is our _own_ sin which defiles us, not our husband's, or anyone else's. Therefore it has to be our sin which we must overcome before we are allowed into heaven. Or we are defiled by our own sins (**Exodus 32:32-33; Matthew 15:16-20; Mark 7: 18-23 & Revelation 21:27**).

The abusive husbands are the wives' opportunity to learn how to conquer their own personal sins (**James 1:1-5 & I Peter Ch. 1-Ch. 4**). Once their sins are conquered, it will be the wives who are on their way to heaven, not their husbands.

Remember? Jesus tells us He will return to reward the work WE do (**Matthew 16:27; 25:1-12, 31-46; Romans 14:11-12; I Corinthians 3:11-15 & Ecclesiastes 11:14**)!

The wives' husbands must do their own work to earn their own reward (**Matthew 25:1-12, 31-46; 22:11-13**). The wives are NOT in their husbands' bodies (**Matthew 25:3-12**).

Therefore, it is up to the husbands to conquer their own sins (**Matthew 25:7-9**).

It is a sacrifice to go out of your way to love your offenders (**Romans 12:1 & Matthew 5:44-48**). These people are hard to love because they haven't treated you with any kindness. But you MUST do something to break your spirit of sin that doesn't want to die (**John 15:12-13**). And getting out of bed in the middle of the night when you do NOT want to, is a good way to break this spirit.

This is what Paul meant when he told us in **Romans 12:1** to present our bodies as a living sacrifice, holy, acceptable unto God, which is our reasonable service. It will take going out of our way and the extra effort to love Jesus' way. He (Jesus) had to go out of His way to love us; thus, we need to do the SAME for Him.

"A new commandment I give unto you, That ye love one another; as I have loved you, that ye also love one another."

John 13:34

"This is my commandment, That ye love one another, as I have loved you. Greater love hath no man than this, that a man lay down his life for his friends."

John 15:12-13

For the people who do not know or understand: to get out of bed and heat up dinner in the middle of the night without the complaining, is presenting your body as a living sacrifice up to God. Getting the cup of coffee when it didn't suite is presenting your body as a living sacrifice up to God. Being pushed out of the way and just forgiving the person who pushed you is presenting your body as a living sacrifice up to God. Forgiving the lady who lived next door and doing the good deeds for her is presenting your body as a living sacrifice up to God.

Are you getting the revelation? Any time you go out of your way to give the "fruits of the Spirit" with a good attitude; this is presenting your body as a living sacrifice up to God. And Paul tells us this is our reasonable service given to Him.

"I BESEECH you therefore, brethren, by the mercies of God, that ye present your bodies a living sacrifice, holy, acceptable unto God, which is your reasonable service."

Romans 12:1

This is also one of the main ways we learn to lay down, kill off, destroy and bury our sin lives for Jesus (**Romans 6:1-6; 12:1, John 13:12-16, 34; 15:12-13; & Matthew 5:38-45**).

Let's return to the wives. You need to know, this kind of loving is required by all of God's true born-again believers, not just the wives. This was just an example of what Jesus means when he tells us we must return love for the hateful acts which have been done to us.

So you don't think that the Holy Spirit is just picking on the wives, let's take one more example. Let's say you are at odds with one of your Christian friends. She offended you by cutting you off in the middle of your conversation not so long ago. When you told her that she hurt your feelings, she was insensitive to your approach. The two of you argued. And you parted company.

You know your offender has children and also has daycare. You also know your enemy is having a hard time with the little ones. To do an act of love would be for YOU to apologize to her for offending her; and to offer to baby sit the children for one day to give your rival a break.

Again, the Holy Spirit knows this act of love is out of your way. It will break into your busy schedule, especially if you deal with children all day long. The Lord does know how you have been mistreated and that you really do not want to help out by taking care of more children.

Besides, you feel as if SHE should apologize to you instead of the other way around. SHE was the one who cut you off in conversation, therefore she sinned against you. And to make matters worse; when you tried to explain to her your problem, she could care less.

However, I cannot express this fact enough; you need to do something to break the back of your disgust for your foe.

It is important. If you do not conquer the sin which lies in **_your heart_** towards your offender, there is a price to pay for not conquering it (**Matthew 12:7; 22:37-40; Exodus 20:1-17; Luke 6:31; John 15:12-13; Romans 2:13; Galatians 5:14; Exodus 32:32-33; Romans 6:23 & Revelation 3:15-16**). Read the scriptures in this order and let them speak to your heart. We must conquer our sins if we seriously want to live with Jesus. This is where we make our choice. Does our Bible promise, and living with Jesus, mean more to us than this life being good on this earth? Or, are our lives on this earth more important? Must we have other people treat us good, and our lives be good on this earth, as according to our standards (**Proverbs 21:2**)? For the person who saves his life on this earth and causes it be good for him personally; he will lose his life with Jesus.

> "For whosoever will save his life shall loose it: and who soever will loose his life for my sake shall find it. For what is a man profited, if he shall gain the whole world, and loose his own soul? . . ."

> **Matthew 16:25-26A**

And we learn to conquer it by going out of our way to do something nice for our antagonist.

What if you win your battle with your friend and she apologizes to you first? What have you gained in God's World (**Matthew 5:46**)? If life is good in this world, you lose your life with Jesus because you don't have to set down on your sin to make things right (**John 12:25**).

It would be your opponent that would have to conquer her sin to be able to apologize to you (**Matthew 5:38-46**). This act would cause you to lose an opportunity to conquer your sin (**Matthew 10: 38-39**) and a new trial would start over again (**John 15: 1-2**). If you are serious about living with Jesus, He will not stop the trials until you learn how to conquer your sin.

> "Every branch in me that beareth not fruit he taketh away: and every branch that beareth fruit, he purgeth it, _**that it may bring forth more fruit.**_"

John 15: 2

One of the ways that we learn to conquer our sin and purge it out of our bodies is by going out of our way to do something nice for our antagonist.

Therefore, to do the extra deed for your adversary is more for you than it is for your opponent. Yes, it requires you to go out of your way to do it, but, it also forces you to break your anger and dislike for your enemies. And this is the beginning of forgiveness.

Once you have forgiven your antagonist, then God can forgive you. It doesn't matter how your opponents or your husband reacts. If they are true believers, they cannot help but to respond to the kindness eventually.

> "Charity never faileth:"

I Corinthians 13:8A

Remember, again, these offenses are being given to you so you can recognize the sins that are still lingering in **your heart**. Once you have been offended, deal with your hurt feelings. (1) Acknowledge them by confessing them to God and Jesus (**I John 1:9**): (2) ask Jesus to dry them up (**Mark 11:12-21**): (3) Cast them out of your body (**Matthew 18:7-9** & **Mark 11:22-24**) and (4) forgive and ask to be forgiven (**Mark 11:25-26** & **Matthew 5:22-25**). Then do the good deed of apologizing and offering to go out of your way to do the deed which means a lot to your opponent.

This is the beginning step in forgiveness. Hang in there. Jesus only has three more steps (**Matthew 5:44B-D**). And if we can get the love down pat, the rest is easy.

We will go into the other steps in our next lesson.

CHAPTER 31

Jesus' Forgiveness IV

I N OUR LAST LESSON the Holy Spirit showed us how Jesus wants us to learn to *love* our offenders. In this lesson He is going to go into Jesus' last three commandments. Just so you know that Jesus' commandment in **Matthew 5:44** is NOT for the women only; in this lesson, the Holy Spirit is going to study these steps from the men's viewpoint. Shall we begin?

> "But I say unto you, Love your enemies, bless them that curse you, do good to them that hate you, and pray for them which despitefully use you, and persecute you;"

> **Matthew 5:44**

Let's say you and another gentleman in your church fell into an argument over the way you believe. You believe **Mark 16:17-18** is for real. But this other gentleman was raised to believe this area of life left when the apostles died off.

> "And these signs shall follow them that believe; In my name shall they cast out devils; they shall speak with new tongues; They shall take up serpents; and if they drink any

deadly thing, it shall not hurt them; they shall lay hands on
the sick, and they shall recover."

Mark 16:17-18

When the discussion began, you stated your belief and the other
gentleman stated his. You know from the bottom of your heart **Mark
16:17-18** does exist in this day and age. Because all of these truths
have happened in your life and including drinking poison by mistake,
you are still around to talk about the experiences. But this man just
will NOT believe you. And he wants to argue his point of view. What
should you do?

Jesus tells us in **Matthew 16:24** & **Mark 8:34** to deny ourselves the
pleasure of the argument. Let your opponent think he is right, and
leave the man standing alone to argue with himself. This is what
Jesus did with His accusers. **Luke 4:16-30** is a perfect example of
this truth. And if we are to follow in His footsteps, then this is what
we are to do as well.

But once you are alone, it is time to deal with all the sin feelings
which would arise during your brief conversation with your foe.

Mister, you must remember, this is the Holy Spirit who is dealing
with you, and not me as a female. It is very hard for me to allow the
Holy Spirit to deal with the men personally because I am a woman.
I want Him to talk to the women or to the men and women together.
To talk to the men only is hard. However I am going to allow the
Holy Spirit to do it, because He needs you to know, Jesus is just as
serious about His instructions for the men as He is for the women.

Just because you are a male, this doesn't mean you don't have the
SAME sin feelings flowing through your body as does the female.

There are resentments, bitterness, grudge holdings, pride, bad thoughts, foolishness, fornications, indignations, feelings of revenge and many other sins which must be addressed for you as well as for the ladies.

Just because you are guys, this fact doesn't mean Jesus is going to let you into heaven without handling your sins. You must be just as serious to do your forgiving as the ladies must be.

Therefore, when you are offended, then you also must acknowledge the fact that you are offended. And then acknowledge the offensive feelings which rise into your minds as well (**Psalm 51:1-7**). You also need to confess your sin feelings to God and Jesus (**I John 1:9**). You need to ask Jesus if He would dry up the roots of your sins (**Mark 11:12-21**). You must cast these sin feelings out of your body (**Matthew 5:29-30; 18:7-9; Mark 9:43-48 & 11:22-24**). And you also must forgive and ask to be forgiven (**Matthew 6:14-15; 18:21-35; Mark 11:25-26 & Matthew 5:22-25**).

Again, you must fill your empty heart with the good deeds of the "fruits of the Spirit". Therefore after you have been offended by your friend at church, you must conclude in your heart that you are going to forgive the man Jesus' way.

Because he is not a member of your personal family you need to go to God and ask Him how He wants you to love the man. Our LORD may tell you to pray **Matthew 13:15** for the man. So, you love your foe by praying for him.

You ask God if He would open your foe's spiritual eyes so He could see that **Mark 16:17-18** was commanded by Jesus. And God and Jesus are not going to take Jesus' truth out of the law ever.

"For verily I say unto you, Till heaven and earth pass, one jot or one tittle shall in no wise pass from the law, till all be fulfilled."

Matthew 5:18

You pray that your foe's spiritual ears would be opened.

"And Jesus answered and said unto him, Blessed art thou, Simon Barjona: for flesh and blood hath not revealed it unto thee, but my Father which is in heaven."

Matthew 16:17

And you pray that God would open up your foe's spiritual heart and understand the scriptures from God and Jesus' viewpoint.

"And the disciple came, and said unto him, Why speakest thou unto them in parables? He answered and said unto them, Because it is given unto you to know the mysteries of the kingdom of heaven, but to them it is not given".

Matthew 13:10-11

When Jesus walked this earth, He prayed **Matthew 13:15** for the Pharisees all the time. We can know He prayed this prayer for the Pharisees because some of them responded to Jesus' prayers. Nicodemus was one of the Pharisees who did respond (**John 3:1-21**). And Nicodemus did change his mind, his heart and his understanding from studying the scriptures from man's viewpoint into understanding and studying the scriptures from God and Jesus' viewpoint.

"For this people's heart is waxed gross, and their ears are dull of hearing, and their eyes they have closed; lest at any time they should see with their eyes, and hear with their ears, and should understand with their heart, and should be converted, and I should heal them."

Matthew 13:15

This is one of the ways you are to complete Jesus' commandment in **Matthew 5:44**. Just so you know; this is the SAME instruction Jesus tells the wives to do for their husbands who are alcoholics and into the pornographic materials on the internet. And this is the SAME instruction Jesus tells the ladies and men to do for their foes who offend them.

In other words, any time you are offended by believers, go to God, and ask our LORD, what kind of prayer does He want you to pray for your offender?

But before you do, again, be sure to do the steps that clear your heart of the sin feelings which rose to the surface of your mind when you were offended. Remember, the whole idea of being offended in the first place, is to cause YOUR sins to rise into your mind so they can be confessed and cleared out of *your body* (**Matthew 18:7-9**).

If you will do this act every time you are offended, you will be surprised at how fast your sins will leave your body (**Mark 11:21-26**). The more you do this, the faster your sins will leave, and when you are totally clear these types of offenses will never trouble you again (**John 15:1-3** & **Romans 6:1-7**).

We have already studied out how we are to do good to them that curse you. You find something that will speak to your enemy's heart and you offer to do the good deed for your enemy. In other words, you do the "fruits of the Spirit" for your foe. You present yourself as a living sacrifice for your foe and you offer to do the good deed (**Romans 12:1**).

Jesus' last instruction is to bless them that curse you. This commandment was left for last because it requires you to work from the scriptures. If you really want your foe to turn around and see things from God and Jesus' viewpoint, it will require ***YOU*** to do your work for God. You need to take the time to find the verses from the Bible that will bless your enemy and write them down.

For an example, if the wives of the alcoholics and the men that are into the pornographic material on the internet, really want good husbands; then they are going to have to take the time to look for the scriptures which will bless their husbands. If you do not know what to look for, ask God to give you the verses that will help your husband. Then go to the concordance and look up the word husband. Read through the scriptures. See which ones will suit you and your husband personally. When you find what you are looking for, write the WORDS over your husband's name. And then start to quote the scriptures out loud.

Husbands, YOU are NOT off of the hook. If you really want your marriage to flourish, you must study as well. ***YOU are the head of your household.*** You are the one who God has called to actually DO the most of the spiritual work in your home.

Mister, whether you know it or NOT your wife DOES NEED you. She needs you to respond to God, and then you and your wife need to make the big decisions according to the Lords' Words.

She needs you to look up in the concordance all the scriptures which pertain to the wives and children. And for YOU to write the scriptures that will bless your family. Then, you also must read them out loud daily. This is BLESSING your own loved ones. You will be surprised at how fast your family will improve.

This replaces the evil with the good (**Matthew 12:33**). You are to confess the evil and rid your body of YOUR sins in the way Jesus instructed you to do in Matthew & Mark.

Sir, your wife really does need you to start your own Bible study for yourself. You see, because you ARE the spiritual leader of YOUR own household, if YOU will turn around and worship GOD and JESUS from YOUR heart; then your whole household will follow after YOUR leadership.

> "Unto the woman he said, I will greatly multiply thy sorrow and thy conception; in sorrow thou shalt bring forth children; and thy desire shall be to thy husband, and *HE shall rule over thee.*"

> **Genesis 3:16**

You see sir, whether YOU like it or not, God did set you as the ruler over your own home. And the children will always follow in your footsteps. This is why Satan is forever after the husband. If he can get the husband to be lazy when it comes to Spiritual matters, then Satan has your children as well!!

It makes it extremely hard for the wife to correct the children. And your living conditions will always be in a poor state of mind. You may survive financially, but there will always be bills. And the children will present problems that will be hard to handle.

It takes the BOTH of YOU to work together and to go to God together. This is WHY, when the lady next door started presenting trouble in the household, it took both husband and wife to combat the dilemma. Whether YOU know it or not, we as wives NEED your help spiritually and physically as well!!

Now as far as looking scripture up and writing it down over the rest of your offenders as Jesus said to do in **Matthew 5:44**, we as humans don't know what to write. If God impresses you to write or say scripture over your offender, then by all means do so.

But if He **doesn't** impress you, then just leave the situation alone. Our LORD is the only ONE who knows your enemies' hearts. And we cannot go against our foes' wills. We can pray that our foes will turn around. But because they are not in our personal families, we don't know what God's promises are for them personally. And we as humans do not know what they need.

When your heart wants the best for your Christian offender, then you can know you have forgiven them from the bottom of your heart!!

And this part of Jesus' work is done. There are many more lessons which need to be learned from Jesus' Words. But if the Holy Spirit can get Y'shua's people to clear their hearts from their own sins this is BIG!!!

> "Every branch in me that beareth not fruit he taketh away: and every branch that beareth fruit, he purgeth it, that it may bring forth MORE fruit. *Now ye are clean through the word which I have spoken unto you.*"

John 15:2-3

If the Holy Spirit can get the people to understand the importance of filling their empty hearts back up with the good works of the "fruit of the Spirit", this is big in God's eyes. If He can get Jesus' people to do the good work of praying, and of doing their own personal BIBLE study, this is also BIG in God's eyes.

Enough is enough. It is time to stop. PRAISE GOD!! Glory to GOD in the Highest!! We are done with this part of our covenant!! And NOW God can bless and prosper the JUST people (**Proverbs 13:22 & 28:13**)!! This is one of our rewards for being faithful to Jesus' Words, and doing this much of God and Jesus' Words!! Amen!